# THE
# SURVIVOR'S
# GUIDE TO
# YOUR
# CAREER
# TODAY

# THE
# SURVIVOR'S
# GUIDE TO
# YOUR
# CAREER
# TODAY

## OLIVER ROLFE

Matador
9 Priory Business Park,
Wistow Road, Kibworth Beauchamp,
Leicestershire, LE8 0RX
Tel: 0116 279 2299
Email: books@troubador.co.uk
Web: www.troubador.co.uk/matador
Twitter: @matadorbooks

ISBN 978 1838591 373

British Library Cataloguing in Publication Data.
A catalogue record for this book is available from the British Library.

Printed and bound in Great Britain by 4edge Limited
Typeset in 10pt Proxima Nova by Troubador Publishing Ltd, Leicester, UK

Matador is an imprint of Troubador Publishing Ltd

*The choices in life are always yours and yours alone.*
*Do not let others define who you are,*
*let YOU define the person*
*you want to become.*

**survivor**
/səˈvʌɪvə/
*noun*
plural noun: **survivor's**

▶ *a person who copes well with difficulties in their life.*

"they are a born survivor"

▶ *a person regarded as resilient or courageous enough to be able to overcome hardship, misfortune, etc.*

**today**
/təˈdeɪ/
Noun

▶ *in this present time.*

**survivor today**
/səˈvʌɪvə/təˈdeɪ/

▶ *a person regarded as resilient or courageous enough to be able to overcome hardship, misfortune and life's difficulties in this present moment.*

# ACKNOWLEDGEMENTS

This book would not have been possible without the help and advice of a number people. In an ever-changing world, we all do our best to make small changes that we hope will add up to make a greater difference.

To Barney, who gave his time for both books. To Sara, who has been an inspiration to me. To Mark, for the support in the early days. To Ruvhen, for his assistance and positivity throughout. To Alan, Kris, Jack and the team, thank you for your support.

To my fantastic family: a wonderful and supportive wife, two beautiful children and our dog. Thank you. I love you all!

To all of you, thank you!

# CONTENTS

# INTRODUCTION

......................................................

After over fifteen years of experience within global executive recruitment and ten years of research for this guide, I am pleased to offer everyone via text, and the medium of YouTube, a set of professional career guidance that uses both video and the written word.

These are aimed at anyone from the age of fourteen years old, all the way through to the end of your career. Within this book and the videos online, topics we will discuss include: how to prepare for an interview; body language in meetings; digital interviews; what interview questions to prepare; how to improve your core energy; a step-by-step meditation guide and much more.

This guide started as a 700-page book that was very close to being published as one piece. At the time, it was literally an A to Z of everything in your career. Within this book, I have selected the very best elements of my research and experiences, which means you only receive the most relevant information for your career.

> *"If you can't fly, run. If you can't run, walk.*
> *If you can't walk, crawl.*
> *No matter what, keep moving."*
> Martin Luther King, Jr.

# ABOUT THE AUTHOR

...................................................................

Oliver Rolfe is Founder and CEO of Spartan International. He focuses on life and career coaching and global equities and investment banking recruitment. Oliver studied accounting and finance and started his career within a leading global accounting firm. Oliver then sought a new challenge and moved into the executive search arena in 2003.

In 2003, he began his financial services recruitment career within a subsidy of S3, one of the largest recruitment companies in Europe. Oliver has spent over fifteen successful years specialising in mid to senior level individuals with outstanding track records in global equities.

In 2010, Oliver founded Spartan Partnership, and later Spartan International Executive Search, which is a global equities executive search firm. Oliver and Spartan remain focused on assisting those in the equities markets globally, both on the buy-side and sell-side of the business.

Oliver has been quoted in *The New York Times*, *Bloomberg*, *The Trade News*, *Gulf Times* and many more global publications. Oliver and Spartan have a daily blog that receives over 600,000 individual views a month, a newsletter with over 13,000 subscribers and a YouTube channel.

His mission has always been: to assist people in becoming the best they can achieve to be.

# THIS IS MY WHY, WHAT IS YOURS?

**This is about understanding and experience.**

**This is a story of success.**

Someone once asked me why I am doing this; my response was and always will be... to help people. This has always been my WHY, my motivation. This is what I believe we are here for, to help each other. That is how we survive, how we evolve, by helping each other.

By laying bare the very essence of what we have all experienced in life, this can be utilised to help many people who feel alone, without knowledge and do not know that others are going through the same experience, whatever that may be. By speaking out we can ALL win and help each other. The time is now!

Whilst I believe I have had a privileged upbringing, none more so than having a loving family and being born in London (UK), I have experienced a number of different events that made a significant and lasting impression on me. All of which have had a very positive affect on my life and have also taught me many important lessons, including a knowing that each experience we have in life has its own message or lesson in it.

For me, these all began when I was five years old...

My parents divorced, something that a very large number of families go through, especially in the Western world. Due to this, I did not spend a huge amount of time with my father growing up. It was really only at thirty, when I had children, that this started to materially change. This time has been great for everyone.

I am fortunate to have a loving mother and grandparents who took the mantle in my early years. My grandfather was an important role model for me, both personally and professionally. I was extremely lucky and I am eternally thankful to them all.

From around the age of six years old to date, I have had over forty-five operations, most of which were general anaesthetics (a major operation at sixteen had left me with minor nerve damage). As someone heavily involved in sports, I had a few injuries that needed other operations: a broken arm, snapped wrist, knee cartilage, ankle and foot operations. I was surprisingly not accident-prone.

I also suffered with asthma, which made it more difficult to play the sports I loved to be involved in daily. I lost quite a bit of time at school as a result of the operations and recovery time. That said, I was always in either the first or second team for every sport I played (about five), usually as captain. It was a responsibility I was privileged to receive, and something I always enjoyed.

In my opinion, great leaders do not lead. People need someone to believe in. Leaders go first and then others follow.

Usually, either for money, belief, passion or a mixture. Leaders shine a light on the path ahead, believing in their convictions and passions. When you follow someone, follow someone you believe in and can respect.

At the age of thirteen, I was what you would call...fat (a word I hate to use), I was around 50lbs heavier than I am now. I was called names, but never harshly. I was always sporty and this helped more than anything else. To be fair, I am not sure I really cared until I was about sixteen, when I started noticing the opposite sex. Being big has always stayed with me and I certainly eat a lot differently now to what I used to eat. My family love to remind me of the number of pizzas and hot dogs I used to eat – what can I say, I like my food. Still do!

During my upbringing, after the divorce of my parents, my siblings had their own personal difficulties. I remember different parts of these times and I am delighted to see the strength, drive and passion of them both, as well as the success it has brought to them.

Around the same time that my siblings were going through their own difficulties, I had a difficult relationship with a girl I loved dearly, who was from another country. After nearly three years of an intense relationship, we separated. It was then, after she had returned home, she told me that she was pregnant and was unsure if it was with my child (something I never believed). Following a confusing and turbulent three years, the truth was revealed and the child was not mine. This was a situation I had to deal with alone at the time. My family was focusing on helping my siblings and I did not want them to have any additional stress. Unfortunately, this had an impact on other relationships around me for some years, until I discovered the truth.

This is something I do not blame anyone for. I have come to realise that we all have our reasons at the time to make certain decisions. We are all still learning; we will always be learning.

Moving on...

At thirty-three I slipped a disc in my back and had to wear a metal brace for six months. This made me look like a poor man's Iron Man, rather than anything else. At that time, I was deeply concerned that I would never be able to carry my children or play with them in the park again. That was a tough moment. The only way to get through those situations is to take one day at a time. We can never look too far in to the future and be obsessed with what might be. We can only ever affect this present moment. This present moment is the ONLY one that exists.

One small step at a time. One foot in front of another.

More recently, it has been found that I have a total of seven damaged discs throughout my spine and I have been told that I have something called Non-Radiographic Ankylosing Spondylitis. This is an inflammatory disease of the spine. This is most certainly another experience to experience. Something to learn and assist others with. I am fortunate to be under very good medical care and will continue to progress positively.

This is the reason why I have chosen to make a donation from the profits of this book to the National Ankylosing Spondylitis Society (NASS), to help them advance their research and assist the many thousands who rely on them daily.

**This is not a sob story. This is a success story.**

I would not change a single experience I have been able to journey through. While I would not want to relive these experiences again, each one of these experiences has made me become the person I am today. That is not something I want to change.

**Why am I describing these personal details about me and my life?**

These experiences, mine or yours, do not define who you are in life; they shape you. They shape you in to the person you can be. You can either choose to be a victim of these experiences or use them to motivate and better yourself, and those around you.

The choices in life are always yours and yours alone. Do not let others define who you are, let YOU define the person you want to become.

**Be positive in everything you do!**

**Choose to be a SURVIVOR!**

# PREPARE TO SUCCEED

*Whatever industry you decide on for your career; make sure you have a passion for it. If you do, you will enjoy it day in, day out.*

# SIMPLE STEPS TO FORMATTING YOUR CV

· · · · · · · · · · · · · · · · · · · · · · · · · · · · · · · · · · · · ·

How do I format a CV? What are the dos and what are the don'ts? CVs can be complicated so it is important to try and simplify them to start with. Here are a few hints and tips to give you some guidance.

## NO LONGER THAN TWO PAGES

Companies do not want to receive a CV that is more than two pages of A4 paper, ideally. Three pages is the maximum that most firms expect.

## YOUR CV ON A WHITE BACKGROUND OR PAPER

Create your CV, whether electronically or physically, using a white background or white paper. Do not use blue, yellow, pink or purple or any other colour. White is absolutely fine.

## KEEP YOUR CV IN A SIMPLE SOFTWARE FORMAT

Keep your CV in a Microsoft Word or PDF format, they are the most simple document formats and are used by everyone. If you change the format into .TXT (plaintext) or .PPT (PowerPoint) for example, it is likely to conflict with a lot of the systems that companies use, as well as recruitment programs. Therefore, those receiving your CV can delete it as quickly as it is received. Some companies will write back asking you for an updated CV, others might not be so generous.

## USE A SIMPLE FONT

Do not go crazy with the font. Keep it simple. For example, use Arial, Times New Roman, Helvetica, Calibri and Verdana, amongst others.

## A PICTURE ON YOUR CV?
## MAKE SURE THAT IT IS A PROFESSIONAL HEADSHOT

Although we do not recommend having a photograph on your CV, if you must have a picture, make sure that it is not too funky, party orientated or sports illustrated. It should be a professional headshot and nothing else.

## BE SUCCINCT

Highlight the major points of focus that you want to promote. The points that someone is going to want to know and be impressed by. This starts from your education all the way through to the present day in your career. By focusing on your key achievements and abilities, it can make your CV stand out from the pack.

## DO NOT LIE!

You will have heard those stories of people being caught out for misrepresentation, as much as five or ten years into their job. It is not worth it. If you are what you are, then you should be where you should be. Do not lie. You will get caught out, sooner or later.

## DO NoT HAvE ANY TyPOS

This is a major no-no: ensure that you do not have any typos or spelling mistakes, your CV is a representation of you, your career and your education. It is your professional life on paper. Make sure there is not a single mistake, as this will reflect negatively on you. It may sound simple but I can guarantee you that every employer will pick up on typos. Automatically it is a huge negative as it shows that you do not care enough, as you have not taken the time to check your CV before submitting it.

. . . . . . . . . . .

For video content on the above, please go to the
Spartan International YouTube channel:
*Simple Steps to Formatting Your CV – https://youtu.be/UiDU62ua-64

# SIMPLE STEPS TO WRITING YOUR COVER LETTER

It is possible that employers in large organisations will not have the time to read a cover letter, however, it is important to ensure you have one and that it sings perfectly to the tune of your career and your professional attributes and successes.

## MAKE SURE IT IS COMPACT

You are already aware that your cover letter may not be read, therefore if it does get read it has to really make an impact. Make sure that you only elaborate on those elements of your personality and career that highlight the very best of you. This is your sales pitch. Keep your cover letter to no more than one page of A4 paper; half of this is more than acceptable.

## BE SPECIFIC TO THE ROLE YOU ARE APPLYING FOR

It is very tempting to write one cover letter and then use the same letter time and time again for every company you approach. If you do this, you could be harming your chances before you have really begun. If you are targeted in your approach, the employing company will recognise your desire to work for them over others who are only wanting a job. Aim to customise your cover letter for each company you apply to. The more understanding, detail and connection you have for the specific company in mind, the higher your chances of receiving an initial interview.

## THE STRUCTURE

For most employers, they are not expecting *War and Peace* from your cover letter, nor are they expecting to read the ramblings of a mad person. It is key to ensure that you have a focus and direction when writing. Know what you want to say and make sure you deliver that message and nothing else.

## WHERE IS IT GOING?

In most cases you will find yourself sending your CV and cover letter to a human resources mailbox or an info@ address. It is important to remember that this is a formal letter and therefore requires it to be addressed accordingly.

## CHECK AND CHECK AGAIN

Bear in mind that your cover letter is going to be the first contact any business has with you. Therefore make sure it is perfect, or as perfect as it can be. Should your cover letter be littered with spelling mistakes, grammatical errors and read as though a child has written it, you might as well throw your CV and cover letter in the bin yourself.

## DO NOT BE AFRAID TO SHINE

When writing a cover letter it is possible you can feel uncomfortable highlighting how wonderful and amazing you profess to be. What is important to remember when writing your letter, this is not you boasting about a mythical fantasy land, this is you highlighting how you can assist, improve and develop a business you would like to join. Be confident in yourself!

# REASONS WHY YOUR CV IS NOT GETTING YOU THE JOB YOU WANT

There are a plethora of reasons why your CV might not get you an interview and can get deleted. Here are a number of hints and tips to ensure that this does not happen to you.

If you take an example such as Goldman Sachs. They receive somewhere in the region of 250,000 graduate CVs every year, with roughly 1% being hired (2,500). This is why you must make the most out of your CV, it has to stand out and be the best it can be.

## MAKE SURE YOUR CV IS EASY TO READ

First and foremost, make sure your CV is easy to read. Is it in the right order? With "education" first, then your professional history. That is what an interviewer or human resources professional expects to see. If they cannot see the information, it is possible they will throw your CV in the bin or delete you. A clear and easy CV to read is as helpful as the information itself.

## IT IS IMPORTANT NOT TO BE GENERIC

Remember that your CV is highlighting the best of you in all your glory. Give the reader of your CV something interesting to read, not only professionally but personally as well. Get them to know you quicker.

## YOU DO NOT HAVE A COVER LETTER

It is possible that you do not have a cover letter – or you have a bad one. Not having a cover letter unfortunately means you are not giving enough of yourself. You are not taking enough time or preparation over your career. Employees and employers all want to have a level playing field, they want to know more about you before you have walked through the door. This is a great way to do it; a well-constructed cover letter can really help if it is done correctly. A poor one can end your chances as you are unlikely to be invited for an interview.

## APPLY FOR THE RIGHT JOB

When you apply for a role, make sure that your personal and professional attributes match the job requirements. Double-check it is the position you want, that it is in the right firm and you know you can add value to that company. In business, everyone is looking for value when hiring, whether this is revenue generation, business connections or an improvement in a business process. If you do not offer value it is almost impossible that you can be hired or a hire can be made.

## YOU ARE NOT RIGHT FOR THE ROLE

Another reason your CV may be rejected is that you are not right for the role. You were never right in the first place and you probably should never have applied. This happens constantly, day after day, all around the world. People apply for jobs they are just not suitable for, and expect an immediate response from the company. In most businesses time is in short supply, so it is imperative you make it easy for everyone, including yourself.

## YOU DO NOT HAVE THE RELEVANT WORK EXPERIENCE

If you want your CV to standout, the best way to do so is by making sure you have taken the correct educational and career steps. As well as a stellar education from a quality school and university, you must also have relevant work experience. Whether your work experience is making the tea/coffee and being a runner or managing a department, what you are demonstrating to a future employer is a passion to learn and work in that specific industry. If you knuckle down and focus during these positions and placements, they can either turn into a job, or give you genuine life and work experience in your chosen industry.

· · · · · · · · · · ·

For video content on the above, please go to the
Spartan International YouTube channel:
*Reasons Why Your CV Is Not Getting You The Job You Want –
https://youtu.be/EGnfBkdX_oM

# DRESS TO IMPRESS

When you dress well, you tend to feel better about yourself. Regardless of this feeling there are certain standards of dress in a professional work setting that must be upheld. The two categories of attire here are "professional dress" and "smart casual dress".

## FOR THE LADIES

### PROFESSIONAL DRESS
*For formal, professional occasions such as a meeting or interview.*

**SUIT** – A suit will consist of a blazer and either skirt or trousers in a matching fabric. These should be kept to the main base colours: black, blue, dark green and tan.

**BLOUSES** – When wearing a blouse, one should ensure that it coordinates with the suit you are wearing. The colours and patterns that can be worn with blouses are vast, for a professional setting it is best to choose a colour that is subtle and matches the suit you are wearing. Avoid wearing blouses that are too tight.

**SMART SHOES** – Close-toed shoes should be worn in a professional environment. Keep shoes limited to brogues, Oxford shoes and heels, which should be kept between two and four inches.

**SKIRTS** – Pencil skirts and A-line skirts are usually the most appropriate for a meeting or interview, ideally knee length or slightly above the knee. These should also be kept to the main base colours of: black, grey, blue and tan.

**DRESSES** – Dresses should not be too long, too short, too tight or too revealing. Much like suits they should be kept to the main base colours with no funky patterns: black, blue, grey and tan.

**JEWELLERY** – Jewellery is a fundamental part of most women's clothing but it is advisable for the jewellery to not be too distracting or too flashy. Ideally no more than one ring on each hand, one set of earrings and a bracelet/watch.

## SMART CASUAL DRESS
*For smart casual dress, usually in the office
and not for meetings*

**BLOUSES** – When wearing a blouse, one should ensure that it coordinates with the suit you are wearing. The colours and patterns that can be worn with blouses are vast, it is best to choose a colour that is subtle and matches the clothing you are wearing. Avoid wearing blouses that are too tight.

**SMART SHOES** – Open toed shoes should be avoided when wearing smart casual attire. Keep shoes limited to flats e.g. brogues, Oxford shoes and heels, which should be kept between two and four inches.

**DRESSES** – Dresses should not be too long, too short, too tight or too revealing. Much like suits they should be kept to the main base colours with no funky patterns: black, blue, grey and tan.

**TROUSERS** – These are suit trousers that have been bought without the accompanying blazer. They are usually worn with these main base colours: black, blue, grey and tan.

**SKIRTS** – Pencil skirts and A-line skirts are usually the most appropriate for the office, ideally knee length or just above the knee. These should also be kept to the main base colours of: black, grey, blue and tan.

**JEANS** – Can be worn with the shoes listed above and should be kept within the remits of black, grey and navy blue.

**JEWELLERY** – Be sure not to be flashy as it can become a distraction.

# FOR THE GENTLEMEN
· · · · · · · · · · · · · ·

## PROFESSIONAL DRESS

For formal, professional occasions such as
a meeting or interview.

**SUIT** – Suits should be limited to three main base colours: black, blue and grey.

**SHIRT** – Shirts should also be kept to two main colours, white and blue (pink is an alternative).

**TIE** – A simple tie with no outlandish colourways or patterns should be worn.

**SMART SHOES** – Keep shoes limited to brogues, Oxford shoes, Derby shoes or monk shoes

**JEWELLERY** – Ideally you should wear no more than one ring, a watch (one metal tone) and a bracelet. Earrings are to be avoided.

## SMART CASUAL DRESS

*For smart casual dress, usually in the office
and not for meetings*

**SHOES** – Shoes to be worn include boat shoes, Chelsea boots, chukka boots, desert boots and loafers.

**SHIRTS** – Shirts should also be kept to three main colours:

white, blue and pink (pastel is acceptable). Can be worn without a tie, preferably keeping a one button down policy.

**SWEATERS** – Often worn with a shirt, you should keep the colours solid if you opt to wear these e.g. black, navy blue and grey.

**BLAZERS** – Should be worn with a shirt, again be careful with the colour selection, making sure that the blazer is not too bright.

**CHINOS** – When worn ensure that you do not branch out of three main base colours: blue, black and brown.

**JEANS** – Can be worn with the shoes listed above and should be kept within the remits of black, grey and navy blue.

**JEWELLERY** – Ideally you should wear no more than one ring, a watch (one metal tone) and a bracelet. Earrings are to be avoided.

# HANDSHAKES AND THEIR SIGNIFICANCE

A handshake is usually the first action that any meeting starts with, and it is something that is surprisingly important. There are a number of different types of handshakes and they communicate certain telltale signs about an individual.

## THE BONE CRUSHER

The bone crusher is a signal for the dominant alpha male/ female. The bone crusher is usually used as a show of dominance, aggression and power. If someone is doing this to you there is very little that you can do; keep it as a competition, keep strong, keep firm and hopefully when you are finished... you will still have a hand left.

## THE SWEATY PALM

No one wants to shake hands with someone with sweaty palms. The last thing you want is for an interviewer or client to be wiping their hand after they have shaken yours. Do yourself a favour, if you do get nervous and you do get a bit sweaty, moments before you go into that meeting room, make sure your hands are quickly dried (a hanky or inside trouser pocket) and then go in for the handshake. Quick, easy and painless.

## THE FINGER CLAMP

This is a handshake that can happen by accident if you come in too early, clamping the fingers rather than the palm of the hand. If this happens, ask for a redo (I do!). If not, it can be a signal of insecurity and someone wanting to keep their distance from you, or a signal of defensive aggression if they are clamping tightly on your fingers.

## THE DEAD FISH

The hand that does not move; the hand that often feels as if there are no bones in it. This indicates that the person is either passive or very reserved. Aim not too squish their hand any further and get out as fast as you can.

## THE SCOOPER

This is the handshake that has no palm to palm contact, almost as though the hand is ready to scoop up the air in-between the two hands. This handshake is one to be wary of, it can either mean that this person is somewhat shy and reserved or that they are not telling you the whole truth. You have been warned!

## THE BRUSH OFF

The brush off is the most negative, rude and arrogant handshake you can have. Going in for a handshake and quickly taking it away is a sign of arrogance; they do not care and they think they are better than the other person.

This is an absolute no-no and something you cannot do at any point. Technically you should never do this anyway, both professionally or personally.

## THE DOLLS HAND

Much like a dolls hand, this is the hand that does not move, is totally rigid and does not grasp the other hand. This handshake can signify someone who is afraid of commitment or, a person that is extremely nervous.

## "THE DONALD"

As you may have seen "The Donald" is overly aggressive, overly firm and does not let go. Not only this, you will see "The Donald" pulling the receiver toward them and again not letting go. This handshake is all about power and command, it sends a clear message saying "I am in control and this is my turf". I can only advise you to use extreme caution at this point.

## THE DOUBLE HANDER

This is a lovely, warm, welcoming handshake. This handshake expresses warmth, friendship, honesty and compassion. This feels as though your hand is being hugged. This is the Rolls Royce of handshakes.

# THE PERFECT HANDSHAKE

..............................................................

1. Make sure your palms are dry

2. Using your right hand, with an outstretched arm

3. Keep direct eye contact

4. Connect fully with the other palm

5. Hold their hand firmly, not in a crushing grip

6. Make sure your hands are side by side and not above to seem controlling

7. Shake for roughly three shakes

8. Let go of their hand and progress to your conversation

............

For video content on the above, please go to the
Spartan International YouTube channel:
*Handshakes & What They Mean – https://youtu.be/xSnsWtSPmTg

# INTERVIEWS AND
# THE PROCESS AHEAD

*Be honest with yourself, be realistic,
stay focused and always be positive.*

# HOW TO SURVIVE THE
# INTERVIEW PROCESS

· · · · · · · · · · · · · · · · · · · · · · · · · · · · · · · · · · · · · · · · · · · · · · · · · · · · · ·

Before you start an interview process there are some aspects to consider ahead of the very first meeting. Remember, giving yourself time to prepare for anything will always give you the extra percent you are looking for and helps you stand out from the crowd. Do not let your competition have that advantage over you; go the extra mile.

## AN INTERVIEW PROCESS CAN BE LENGTHY

It is possible that an interview process can be lengthy at times, especially as you progress through your career. It can be that the interviews are going to be conducted over days, weeks and possibly even months.

## YOU ARE LIKELY TO MEET MANY
## INTERVIEWERS

It is extremely likely that you will be meeting a number of people in the interview process. If you think of the likes of Google, Goldman Sachs and Apple for example, they are famed for having between six and twelve interview rounds. Be prepared and get yourself mentally ready for a long process.

## CONDUCT YOUR OWN RESEARCH

Before any meeting, especially your first with someone new, you should conduct your own research. This is to make sure you have knowledge of the company, the department, where they are looking to develop, where you may fit and, most importantly, where you can add value. Additionally, you will want to know everything you possibly can about the person on the other side of the table at a meeting; this is something that you need to do and will certainly give you an advantage over other candidates.

## REMEMBER THAT EVERY
## INTERVIEW IS BRAND NEW

It is essential to remember that every single interview is brand new. Should you find yourself having been in the same room and building for hours, remember, for everyone that walks through the door and sits opposite you, it is a brand new meeting. At this moment, you must mentally *reset* and *start afresh*. At best, any interviewer that walks through the door may have had a small amount of feedback from the interviews beforehand, nevertheless you cannot make that assumption.

## DO NOT LET GOOD FEEDBACK
## GO TO YOUR HEAD

Whether it is throughout an interview process or a set of client meetings, do not let good feedback go to your head. Stay composed and stay focused. Use it as motivation for the next round of meetings, rather than thinking that the position or objective is already yours. As soon as you allow your ego to take over you will not give the best version of yourself.

· · · · · · · · · · ·

For video content on the above, please go to the
Spartan International YouTube channel:
*How to Survive The Interview Process – https://youtu.be/4jPrlo6xE-E

# INTERVIEW QUESTIONS YOU MUST PREPARE

Throughout any interview process, whether for a new position in the same company or one elsewhere, there are some specific and key questions that always arise. By preparing for these questions it will assist you in the delivery of your answers, as well as your confidence ahead of the meeting. Fail to prepare, prepare to fail!

## WHY ARE YOU LEAVING YOUR CURRENT ROLE?

The reason why you are being asked this is to ascertain if you are an unreliable person and someone who is looking to move from role-role, rather than have a fully-fledged career within that company and position. It is important that you think of a good reason why you are moving on from your current position.

## WHY SHOULD WE HIRE YOU AND WHAT MAKES YOU BETTER THAN ANYONE ELSE?

This is designed for the interviewer to understand your motivations, your drive and whether you can show a genuine appetite and excitement for this job. Any company interviewing wants to know that the individual on the other side of the table is as passionate about the role as they are. It is important from the ground up to be absolutely dedicated in everything you do; if you do not have a passion for what you do, maybe it is time to look for a new position or even a new industry.

## WHY DO YOU WANT THIS POSITION IN THIS PARTICULAR COMPANY?

This question is asked to understand your true motivation for wanting this position; whether you are looking for a long-term career within the company or a short-term fix to pay the bills. With this question, you are being asked for examples and evidence of why you want to be part of the culture and advancement of the business. If you can demonstrate that you have a passion for the job and an understanding of the company, you are more likely to be successful.

## WHAT WOULD YOUR COLLEAGUES SAY ABOUT YOU?

The real reason you are being asked this question is to identify your strengths and weaknesses, and whether there are any you can highlight yourself and share with the interviewer. Now, a well thought out and planned answer is best to really highlight some key strengths you can offer for this position, ideally from your professional and personal life. This is a perfect opportunity to shine in an interview.

## TELL ME ABOUT A SITUATION YOU COULD HAVE HANDLED DIFFERENTLY

Towards the end of an interview process this question comes up more and more. The reason you are being asked this is to understand your ethical compass and whether you are a person that is likely to get on well with the rest of the team and department.

## WHAT ARE YOUR GREATEST ACCOMPLISHMENTS?

This is a question to understand more about yourself and to potentially identify some new revenue streams that could be utlitised in the company, should you join them. At this stage, do not be shy to explain some of your business ideas or strategies, being wary not to give too much away.

## DO YOU HAVE ANY QUESTIONS FOR ME?

This is a completely open-ended question and it is an opportunity to ask the interviewer anything you want to know, on a professional level. It is also an opportunity for you to start an open conversation and for them to get to know you better. If your question hits the right cord and strikes an interest, you will both start to get to know each other effortlessly. This is a great opportunity to get to know your interviewer and, hopefully, future boss or colleague.

. . . . . . . . . . .

For video content on this topic, please go to the
Spartan International YouTube channel:

*Interview Questions & What They Mean – https://youtu.be/oOlyW48i9aY

# THE INTERVIEW: THE QUESTIONS

In this section you will be able to prepare and practice a plethora of possible questions you may be asked in an interview situation. Preparing for the questions below will most certainly assist you in your interview processes.

It is useful to mark or keep a note of those questions you find difficult to answer; you can spend additional time practicing these at your leisure.

## ABOUT YOU

1. Tell me about your career.
2. Discuss your CV.
3. Talk me through your educational background.
4. Which was your preferred class at university?
5. Why did you choose your university?
6. Why did you choose your university course?
7. What are your strengths?
8. What are your weaknesses?
9. What is your passion?
10. What gets you up every morning?
11. Where do you see yourself in five years?
12. What sort of person are you?

13. Describe yourself?
14. Tell me about yourself?
15. Are you a trustworthy person?
16. Do friends trust you with their secrets?
17. What is success for you?
18. What motivates you in life?
19. What do you wish for before you sleep?
20. What are your career goals?
21. How do you handle pressure?
22. What did you eat last Tuesday for lunch?
23. What did you do at the weekend?
24. What would bring you contentment?
25. What makes you uncomfortable?
26. Who is your mentor?
27. Who is your role model?
28. What can you offer us that someone else cannot?
29. How will you improve our team?
30. Do you believe that you are a good fit for us?
31. Are we a good fit for you?
32. Are you willing to relocate?
33. Are you willing to travel?
34. Are you comfortable with flexible working?
35. Can you work from home?
36. Are you disciplined?
37. Would you work holidays/weekends?
38. Would you work 40+ hours a week?
39. When can you start with us?
40. Talk me through a time you failed.
41. Tell me about a time you made a mistake.
42. What has been your biggest failure?

43. Can you talk about a mistake you made in the past, and how you overcame it?
44. Can you talk about a challenge you faced in the past? How did you overcome it?
45. Can you tell me a time when you failed to meet a deadline?
46. What is more important – deadlines or the quality of work?
47. Can you give an example of a time you streamlined a process?
48. Give a time when you went above and beyond the requirements for a project.
49. How would you deal with an angry or irate customer?
50. What are your salary requirements?
51. What was your last bonus?
52. Were you well paid in your previous role?
53. What is your notice period?
54. Do you have any stock or bonus to buy out?
55. Do you have a company car?
56. Do you need a company car?
57. What was the last book you read for fun?
58. What was the last book that inspired you?
59. What are your hobbies?
60. What is your favourite website?
61. What is your favourite podcast/TV show?
62. Talk me through a time you had a moral dilemma.
63. Talk me through a time when you helped someone.
64. Tell me how you handled a difficult situation?
65. Are there enough hours in the day?
66. What is the biggest decision you have made in your life?
67. Would you say you are a perfectionist?
68. What have you done professionally that you are most proud of?

69. Tell me about a personal accomplishment you are proud of?

70. Who is the most famous and influential person you would want to meet and why?

71. Who is the most famous and influential person you have met with?

72. Who is your hero?

73. What would you say to your hero if you met them?

74. What questions have I not asked you?

75. Do you have any questions for me?

## ABOUT THE COMPANY YOU ARE INTERVIEWING FOR

1. How did you hear about this position?

2. What do you know about us?

3. What do we do here?

4. What year was our inception?

5. How long have we been in operation?

6. Why our firm?

7. Why are you interested in working for us?

8. How did you research us before this interview?

9. What is our current share price?

10. What is the name of our CEO?

11. What is our company motto?

12. How many people work here?

13. How many locations do we have?

14. Which location would be best for you, and why?

15. Which department do you want to work within?

16. Which department would best suit your skillset?

17. What is likely to impact us in terms of recent financial news?

18. Why are you right for us?
19. Why are we right for you?
20. Why should I/we hire you?
21. Why do you want this job in our company?
22. What exactly do you expect to do in this role?
23. What skills do you think are required to do this job?
24. Why do you want to work for this role in this division?
25. Which of your skills and experiences make you appropriate for this job?
26. What have you achieved that makes you suitable for this role?
27. What would you accomplish in the first thirty/sixty/ninety days on the job?
28. What do you like the most and least about working in this industry?
29. Do you know anyone who works for us?
30. Have you met/spoken with any employee of our firm previously?

## INDUSTRY COMPETITORS

1. Which other companies have you applied to? Why do you want to work for us instead of them?
2. Who are our competitors?
3. How do you rate our rivals?
4. What makes us different from our competitors?
5. Would you not be better suited to working for another organisation?
6. Who are the top three to five companies in our sector?
7. If you could buy one of those companies, which would it be and why?

8. Who is our biggest competitor?
9. Which global regions do our competitors focus on?
10. What is our market share compared to others in the industry?
11. What is our market strategy compared to theirs?
12. If you were our CEO, what strategy would you use?
13. What products/services do our competitors have that we do not?
14. Where are our core strengths ahead of our rivals?
15. In what sectors are our competitors stronger than us?

## CURRENT EMPLOYMENT

1. Talk to me about your current job.
2. What is most fulfilling about your current job?
3. What is most boring?
4. Do you get on with your boss?
5. Do you get on with your team?
6. Is it a good place to work?
7. Is it a pleasant environment?
8. Do you feel valued?
9. What is your dream job?
10. Is there anything you can change rather than leave?
11. Is there another department you can move to?
12. Why do you want to leave your current company?
13. Would you consider a counter offer from them?
14. Can they tempt you to stay with them?
15. Why are you looking for a new job?
16. What would your direct report say about you?
17. What are your bosses' strengths/weaknesses?

18. If I called your boss right now and asked them what is an area that you could improve on, what would they say?
19. What are three things your former manager would want you to improve on?
20. What are your co-workers' pet peeves?

## PREVIOUS EMPLOYMENT

1. Talk to me about your previous jobs.
2. Which was your most fulfilling job?
3. Which was the most boring?
4. Did you get on with your bosses?
5. Did you get on with your colleagues?
6. Was it a good place to work?
7. Was it a pleasant environment?
8. Would you work at your previous company in the future, given the opportunity?
9. How did you impact your former company?
10. What was your most memorable day in your previous company, and why?

## TEAM WORK AND LEADERSHIP

1. Which role do you usually take in a team?
2. Do you prefer to sit back, lead or follow?
3. Talk to me about a time when you dissuaded a colleague from making a bad decision.
4. Tell me about a time when you had to persuade someone to do something they did not want to do.

5. If you disagree with a team member, how do you find a solution?

6. Describe a time when you worked in a team where there were disagreements.

7. Tell me about a time when you disagreed with your boss? How did you move past this?

8. What would your teammates say about working with you?

9. Do you work well within a team?

10. Do you prefer to work alone?

11. Do you work better in a team or alone?

12. Give an example of a time you acted as a leader.

13. What are some of your leadership experiences?

14. Would you consider yourself a natural leader?

15. Give an example of you being a natural leader.

16. How would you let someone go from a job?

17. Talk to me about a time when you were a follower rather than a leader.

18. Are you a leader or a follower?

19. Why would your teammates choose to work with someone else instead of you?

20. Would you rather be captain of a losing team or the regular member of a winning team?

# BRAIN TWISTING
# QUESTIONS

It is possible that in an interview situation you could be asked a brain teasing question. This is often to see how you react when under pressure, and, for the interviewer to assess how your mind works logically. Below are some examples of infamous brain twisters. (All questions are available from multiple sources, including YouTube and the internet).

## WHAT BRAIN TWISTERS ARE YOU LIKELY TO COME ACROSS?

1.  How many plastic bottles were sold in the UK last year? (Estimation question)

2.  How many times in a day are the hands of a clock at right angles? (Answer: forty-four)

3.  At 3:30pm what is the angle between the hands of a clock? (Answer: seventy-five degrees)

4.  What is your opinion about Adolf Hitler?

5. Tell me an interesting story.

6. You studied history at university. So, are you going into finance for the money?

7. How many windows are in this building? (Estimation)

8. What is the sum of numbers from 1 to 100? (Answer: 5050)

9. A sundial has the fewest moving parts of any timepiece. Which has the most? (Answer: an hourglass, with thousands of grains of sand)

## THE BONUS BRAIN TWISTER – ONE OF THE FAVOURITES

10. What makes this number unique – 8,549,176,320? (Answer: it contains each number, from zero through nine, in alphabetical order)

# MIND BENDING QUESTIONS

..................................................

Whilst it is unlikely that you will be asked a fully fledged Mind Bending Question off the top of your head in an interview, it is very possible that an interviewer could ask you to complete a select number of questions, tasks and mind benders in a set time frame to assess how you react under pressure. The following Mind Benders are some of the most popular and 'fun' questions that could possibly arise in an interview process. Let the games begin!

**You have 100 balls (fifty black balls and fifty white balls) and two buckets. How do you divide the balls into the two buckets so as to maximise the probability of selecting a black ball if one ball is chosen from one of the buckets at random?**

**Answer:**

Being clear, you are assuming that one of the two buckets is chosen at random and then one of the balls from that bucket is chosen at random. You want to put one black ball in one of the buckets and all of the other ninety-nine balls in the other bucket. This gives you just slightly less than a 75% chance of having a black ball chosen. The maths works as follows: there's a 50% chance of selecting the bucket containing one ball with a 100% chance of selecting a black ball from that bucket. And a 50% chance of selecting the bucket containing ninety-nine balls with a 49.5% (49/99) chance of selecting a black ball from that bucket. Total probability of selecting a black ball is (50% * 100%) + (50% * 49.5%) = 74.7%.

**Three envelopes are presented to you by an interviewer. One contains a job offer, the other two contain rejection letters. You pick one of the envelopes. The interviewer then shows you the contents of one of the other envelopes, which is a rejection letter. The interviewer now gives you the opportunity to switch envelope choices. Should you switch?**

**Answer:**

The answer is yes. Say your original pick was envelope A. Originally, you had a 1/3 chance that envelope A contained the offer letter. There was a 2/3 chance that the offer letter was either in envelope B or C. If you stick with envelope A, you still have the same 1/3 chance. Now, the interviewer eliminated one of the envelopes (say, envelope B), which contained a rejection letter. So, by switching to envelope C, you now have a 2/3 chance of getting the offer and you have doubled your chances.

Note that you will often get this same question but referring to playing cards (as in 3-Card Monte) or doors (as in Monte Hall/ Let's Make a Deal) instead of envelopes.

**Four people need to cross a bridge at night to get to a restaurant. They have only one flashlight and seventeen minutes to get there. The bridge must be crossed with**

**the flashlight and can only support two people at a time. Person A can cross in one minute, Person B can cross in two minutes, Person C can cross in five minutes and Person D takes ten minutes to cross. How can they all make it to the restaurant on time?**

**Answer:**

First, Person A takes the flashlight and crosses the bridge with the Person B. This takes two minutes. Person A then returns across the bridge with the flashlight taking one more minute (three minutes passed so far). Person A gives the flashlight to Person C, Person C and Person D cross together taking ten minutes (thirteen minutes passed so far). Person C gives the flashlight to Person B, who re-crosses the bridge taking two minutes (fifteen minutes passed so far). Person A and Person B now cross the bridge together taking two more minutes. Now, all are across the bridge at the restaurant in exactly seventeen minutes.

**You are given a three-gallon jug and a five-gallon jug. How do you use them to get four gallons of liquid?**

**Answer:**

Fill the five-gallon jug completely. Pour the contents of the five-gallon jug into the three-gallon jug, leaving two gallons of liquid in the five-gallon jug. Next, dump out the contents of the three-gallon jug and pour the contents of the five-gallon jug into the three-gallon jug. At this point, there are two gallons in the three-gallon jug. Fill up the five-gallon jug and then pour the contents of the five-gallon jug into the three-gallon jug until the three-gallon jug is full. You will have poured one gallon, leaving four gallons in the five-gallon jug.

**A car travels a distance of sixty miles at an average speed of 30mph. How fast would the car have to travel the same sixty-mile distance home to average 60mph over the entire trip?**

**Answer:**

Most people say 90mph, but this is actually a trick question! The first leg of the trip covers sixty miles at an average speed of 30mph. So, this means the car travelled for two hours (60/30). In order for the car to average 60mph over 120 miles, it would have to travel for exactly two hours (120/60). Since the car has already travelled for two hours, it is impossible for it to average 60mph over the entire trip.

# VIDEO AND DIGITAL INTERVIEWS

. . . . . . . . . . . . . . . . . . . . . . . . . . . . . . . . . . . . . . . . . . . . . . . . . . . . . . . . . . . . . . .

Video and digital interviews are happening more frequently as the professional world has become increasingly global and technology based in recent years. Additionally, it can also quicken an interview process and save on costs, should there be more than one office location or someone is out of the country.

Digital interviews should be approached in the same manner as a face-to-face interview, with some subtle differences. Take some time to prepare for a digital interview and be aware of the potential pitfalls to avoid.

## FIND A SUITABLE LOCATION

Before the interview starts you should find a suitable location to set up your device. It is best to find a quiet room where you will not be disturbed by outside noise or interference. Set up the device facing a blank wall with nothing behind you, no posters and no view of the room. The only aspect you want the interviewer to focus their attention on, is you.

## EQUIPMENT TO USE

Fortunately, in this day and age, most smart phones have the capacity to conduct a video conference call. Similarly with most tablets, laptops and desktops. Ideally, you want to use a device that you can either set firmly on a table or stand and that is at eye level. You do not want to be holding your device or camera whilst the meeting is taking place. This is a huge no-no. Make sure that there is either enough battery remaining for the duration of your call, or that it is plugged in to a power source.

## CHECK YOUR INTERNET CONNECTION

This is a simple and pivotal exercise to undertake. Internet or Wi-Fi connection is one of the biggest difficulties to overcome within digital interviews. If either yours or the interviewer's connection is weak, it is likely to impact the interview dramatically. If either party is unable to hear complete questions or sentences it is unlikely there will be an understanding between the two. Should you find yourself in this situation after an interview has begun, it is recommended that you highlight this to the interviewer immediately, with a view to fixing the connection or rescheduling the digital meeting. Do not sell yourself short.

## WEAR THE CORRECT ATTIRE

Take note, this is exactly the same as a face-to-face interview. Dress like it! Whilst it is likely that your bottom half will not be in view of the interviewer, it is important to dress properly. It is possible that the interviewer may ask you to show them some examples of your work, or you may want to get some paper etc. Additionally, if you dress in the correct manner you will feel more confident and focused.

## PRACTICE MAKES PERFECT

It is possible that you may not be comfortable speaking into a camera or screen, although this is something that is changing rapidly with the rise of smart phones. If so, it will increase your confidence if you spend some time in front of the camera practicing interview scenarios. Speaking with friends or family members via video-phone can also be a big boost for your confidence and an easy practice session.

## TAKE A DEEP BREATH AND ENUNCIATE

Moments before the conversation begins, take three to five long, deep breaths – do not rush. This will help calm your nerves and desist you from speaking at 100mph as soon as the conversation begins. Concentrate initially on speaking slowly and clearly, until you find your own rhythm and volume level. Pronounce your words and aim to ensure that you are heard clearly and concisely.

## KEEP YOUR FOCUS AND CONNECT

Connecting with your interviewer on a personal level can prove to be slightly more challenging via video conference than in person. It is therefore important that you maintain your focus and eye contact during the meeting. The best way to do this is to focus on the camera itself, rather than the screen. By focusing your eye contact on the camera you will come across as engaged and focused. Do not let yourself wander during the conversation.

## MAINTAIN A GOOD POSTURE, RELAX AND SMILE

Throughout your conversation, remember to maintain a good posture and do not let yourself slouch. You may not be sat around a boardroom table, however, you should mentally prepare this way. Enjoy your conversation and where it takes you. The more you enjoy it, the more you will feel comfortable, smile and be yourself. Have fun, relax and do your best. You cannot ask anymore of yourself.

# PHONE INTERVIEWS

Phone interviews have been happening for many years. A phone interview can often be challenging for people, especially when you are not used to it. When you are face-to-face you have a different interaction with an individual; you feel them energetically, you connect with them, you can see how they react to your questions and to what you are saying. Sometimes over the phone you can lose an element of communication due to a non-visual connection with a person. This is something you need to gain back on a phone interview. Try your best to get yourself across as positively as possible.

## PREPARATION AND REPETITION

To start with, it is useful to have a practice. Should you apply directly for an interview, use a friend or a colleague to run through a few practice questions and get used to answering these types of questions over the phone. If you are working with a headhunter on this position, I am sure they will be willing to give you practice questions and run you through an interview scenario (*Go to Interview Questions on page 26*).

## CHOOSE THE RIGHT DATE AND TIME

A few days ahead of the interview, double-check you have booked the call at the right time, on the right date and you know what you are interviewing for and where. Additionally, it helps to know who you are speaking with and everything about that person and the department they work in.

## FIND A QUIET LOCATION

Ahead of the conversation, make sure you find yourself a quiet room. Ensure you are not going to be disturbed by any outside noise, anyone coming in, or knocking at the door. The last thing you want is to be interrupted mid-sentence, being putting off your stride and losing your train of thought.

## HAVE KEY INFORMATION IN FRONT OF YOU

It is always recommended having a pad of paper and pen, some notes on the interviewer and the company, as well as your CV to hand. This way it is useful to run through everything together and you will not have a problem remembering any details.

## STAND UP AND TALK

Personally, one of my favourite things to do on the phone, especially when interviewing, is standing up. When you stand up your voice changes, you are enabled to emote better, you are able to get your voice across better with differing tonalities that exhibit passion and presence in a conversation. Sometimes when you are sitting down, your voice changes and can come across as having a lack of energy and enthusiasm. It is vital that your voice is light, lifted and positive. This will ensure that your voice is heard clearly, whilst being able to demonstrate your passion.

## BREATHE! TAKE YOUR TIME

Make sure that you do not rush what you are saying. Take your time and remember that it is not a race. Speak as though you are sitting in front of someone face-to-face and do not fear the phone. Wait for your turn to speak and aim not to interrupt the other person at any time.

## DRESS THE PART

An odd tip, which is something a lot of people do not do, dress well for a phone interview. Your mentality changes when you wear something more professional or when you wear something smarter to go out. The same relates to your tone when you are wearing a suit, shirt and tie etc. for an interview, even if this happens to be a phone interview. If you end up feeling more presentable you will sound more confident, be more professional and give a better delivery.

## DO NOT EAT, DRINK OR CHEW GUM

There are some really important no-no's during a phone interview. First and foremost, do not chew gum, do not eat and try not to drink. If you need a sip of water; take the phone away from you so that the other person cannot hear, take a sip and then come back. The same applies if you have a cough, sniff or the need to sneeze. Do not sneeze down the phone, no one wants to hear that. If you do sneeze take your time, apologise, say excuse me and move on.

## TRY NOT TO FILL SILENCES

When you are on the phone it is possible to feel uncomfortable, especially around silences. Try not to fill these silences, unless you have something to say. If you are asked a question by an interviewer and want to answer quickly because of the silence, do not. Say to the interviewer, "Please let me take a moment to think about this." This way, the interviewer knows exactly what you are doing. There are no uncomfortable silences and it gives you time to think so that you can deliver the perfect message and the right answer.

. . . . . . . . . . .

For video content on the above, please go to the
Spartan International YouTube channel:
*Phone Interviews – https://youtu.be/S5Xztu07ERE

# HOW TO RESIGN WITH STYLE AND DIGNITY

*In life, you either win or you learn. Every experience is either a chance to progress and learn, or to repeat past lessons missed.*

# RESIGNATION PREPARATION

Resigning from a job can feel like a very unnatural place to be, especially when you have enjoyed the time at your current place of work. If you are ready to resign you have obviously made up your mind about leaving the company. Before taking that final plunge, there are some important elements to consider.

## THE DAY OF YOUR RESIGNATION

Make sure you are ready for the day ahead. Be 100% confident with your decision and be committed in your approach. You want to resign and leave your current position without any legal, professional or personal ramifications. In short, you want to leave with the least fuss or complications. It is quite possible that your paths may cross again sometime in the future.

## WITH WHOM DO YOU RESIGN?

This is a point of contention for many people. To be 100% sure of your exit, the best way in which to resign is to prepare two copies of your signed resignation letter. When you first arrive at work, hand one letter directly to your company's HR department. The other letter should be personally handed to your direct boss or their superior if they are not available. This will ensure that the formal process must legally begin.

## THE RESIGNATION MEETING

During the meeting you have five clear goals to establish:

1. *Control the meeting*
2. *Why are you resigning*
3. *Create and maintain a friendly atmosphere*
4. *Confirm your exit date and contractual obligations*
5. *Agree next move*

## GETTING YOUR WORDS AND ATTITUDE RIGHT

Your goals on your resignation day are fixed and firm, you should not be swayed from them. Bear in mind at all times that you should be polite, respectful and never – unless you cannot help it – "burn your bridges" in terms of resigning. You should stay professional and non-personal where possible.

## THE STARTING GUN

▶ *"I wanted to let you know that I have decided to take another job opportunity. I have enjoyed my time here and thank all whom I have worked with. Now, how do we make this transition a positive one?"*

Once you have said those words: "I am handing in my notice" or "I am resigning from the company", the battle for control of your career begins. You want to move on and start your new career. Now you have changed the relationship and you are in the driving seat. If they get you to consider a possible counter offer, they are taking control back from you. At this stage, a business could be in a position where they cannot afford to let you go under any circumstance, in this instance a counter offer could be extremely intriguing. Remember they have two objectives:

▶ *To re-establish control over your career*

▶ *To get out of their personal failure. (When your boss goes to the management meeting, their peers will say "How did you manage to lose such an important member of the team, they were great.")*

## THE POSSIBLE COUNTER OFFER

When you accept an offer of employment for a new job, the deal is still not closed, as you still have to resign and exit from your current company formally. *See the next chapter on Counter Offers for more information.*

## THE COMPANY PARTY LINE AND NEXT STEPS

When you resign it is likely that your existing company will say one or more of the following:

▶ *"Congratulations, complete your notice period and good luck."*

▶ *"Clean out your desk and leave this afternoon,"* in which case you will be on *"gardening leave"* during your notice period.

*Or they will say, "Hold off on your decision for [a number of] days; let us talk to you once more." This is the most likely scenario and is effectively buying for time while they try and find out more and work out their next steps.*

A number of other "stalling tactics" that might be said are:

▶ *"The Managing Director is coming in and will surely want to talk to you."*

▶ *"We did not want to tell you about your new promotion until next quarter however..."*

▶ *"We have plans for a new project and we have a special role for you to play."*

In most instances these are all situations that probably would not have been said had you not forced their hand and do not therefore constitute the basis for a sensible and trusting on-going relationship.

## LEAVE IN THE BEST WAY POSSIBLE

Whatever you do, no matter how difficult, try to leave your current company having followed the correct procedures.

By doing this you will be able leave with your head held high and with your respect and professional reputation intact. Aim for there to be the smoothest of transitions possible and to complete all open assignments, projects and tasks requested of you before your final leaving date. This will also ensure that you receive a positive reference letter, should you require one in the future and that the door is always left open for you.

**Make sure you leave on the best possible terms and do not burn bridges.**

# THE COUNTER OFFER

Most people say "my company will not make a counter offer". Deep inside they are expecting, or at least hoping to get one, if only for ego gratification. Whether this is something you are expecting or not, it is certainly worth while preparing yourself for the potential scenario.

## THE POSSIBLE COUNTER OFFER

When you accept an offer of employment for a new job, the deal is still not closed, as you still have to resign formally. As you are a valued employee your current company is unlikely to want to lose you and could put some pressure on you to stay. This is likely to be through one or more of the following:

1. *A financial counter offer*
2. *A new title*
3. *A promotion*
4. *Peer pressure*
5. *Expressions of love and respect*

## WHY DO COMPANIES MAKE A COUNTER OFFER?

Companies realise that it is less expensive to give a little extra money, respect and a title to keep an existing employee than it is to pay a fee to hire a new employee (who will probably come in at a higher salary). They will also be aware of the time and effort of recruiting externally. That said, none of these in the long-term will make up for the reasons you were open to moving in the first place. None of them take into account the challenge or potential of the new role.

## YOU CANNOT TURN BACK TIME

Once the cat is out the bag, you cannot unsay what has already been said. This is something to be wary of: once you have made it known that you wish to leave, that does not change, even if you stay. This is one of the reasons that counter offers rarely work out, the trust between the two parties has been damaged and in a number of cases, broken. In certain circumstances the line manager can be changed, creating a small window of opportunity for future relationships.

## BE AWARE OF THE IMPOSSIBLE OFFER

It is possible that in a moment of panic and irrational thinking, your current company or line manager may offer you something that is so hard to turn down as it is too good to be true. Often in this instance, that turns out to be exactly the situation. Whether this is a financial package that is unachievable, or a new title in a new department that has no funding. Whatever is put in front of you, make sure that it is rock solid, legally binding and very much in writing and signed by the most senior member of staff possible.

## REMEMBER THE REASONS YOU RESIGNED

Whatever happens during your resignation process, one thing is for sure, you wanted to leave your company for one reason or another. The chances are that any counter offer from your current company will not amend or change the reasons for you wanting to seek employment elsewhere. Before accepting any counter offer, ask yourself: why did they not make these offers to me before I resigned? Has anything fundamentally changed? Do I still want to leave?

# POINTS OF CONFUSION
# AND LEGAL ISSUES

When resigning from a company there are often points of confusion that almost always arise. To prepare yourself ahead of time, here are a select number of points to be mindful of before the big day. Remember, it is imperative that you understand all of the terms, conditions and restrictions of your current employment contract ahead of handing in your resignation.

## YOU DO NOT HAVE TO LET THEM KNOW WHERE YOU ARE GOING

Your boss will want to know where you are going, in what capacity and for how much. You are not obliged to tell them any of this information (whatever they say) and it may give them fuel with which to "rubbish" your new employer.

## GARDENING LEAVE CAN BE MUTUALLY NEGOTIATED

Gardening leave *can* be negotiable. If you are on one, three, six or twelve months' notice provisions, it is fine to try and negotiate this down to a mutually agreeable level. It is possible that by reducing the notice period you will also forego any money for this period. You may feel that you want to start your new role sooner, or have been incentivised to do so. In the long-term it is usually worth getting out as quickly as possible and into your new role.

## DO NOT FEEL PRESSURED TO GIVE AWAY INFORMATION

You are not obliged to tell your existing company how you found your new job, whether you were contacted directly by the company or via a recruiter. If you are working with a head-hunter, they can give you more advice on this in each specific instance.

## YOU ARE NOT COMPELLED TO DO MORE THAN CONTRACTUALLY OBLIGED

You are never obliged to work more than your notice period, even if this means a project you are part of when you resign suffers. The notice period is designed to give the company time to organise these details and it is not something you need to concern yourself with.

## LEAVE IN THE MOST POSITIVE WAY POSSIBLE

Whilst on your notice period, you are obligated to act responsibly and in the best interests of the company you are leaving. You should not, during this period, be disruptive, persuade other staff to leave or not bother to do any work you have been assigned to do – your existing company will remember these last few weeks and judge you in the future on this.

## RESPECT YOUR CURRENT COMPANY

You must respect your company's wishes vis-à-vis what to say to existing clients whilst you are still an employee and when you have left the firm. You will still be legally and professionally bound by a code of conduct. In short, do not bad-mouth your existing company either on the way out or when you have left. It is never worth it and can often cause potential issues down the road for you.

## DO NOT WORK BEFORE YOU OFFICIALLY START

You must not do any work for your future employer whilst in your notice period (unless expressly agreed by your existing employer). This could open up a can of worms and cause you an issue for very little gain. Follow the rules and guidelines of the contract you willingly signed and agreed too.

## ALWAYS BE AWARE OF YOUR CONTRACTUAL OBLIGATIONS

You must abide by any long-term confidentiality clauses in your contract and any other terms referred to regarding leaving the company. You have been warned!

# RESIGNATION LETTER FORMAT

These example letters can be used as templates for how to resign in writing in the most professional and effective manner.

## EXAMPLE 1 – THE HELPFUL HANDOVER

Name
Address

Date

Dear (add name of your boss),

I would like to inform you that I am leaving (add name of present employer). This was a difficult decision, as working for (add name of present employer) has been a positive experience and one for which I am thankful. I have learned a lot here, and have enjoyed working with you and the team.

However, after due consideration, I have decided to accept a position with a new employer that exactly meets my career plans. This decision was reached after thorough consideration of both opportunities and career prospects.

I wish continued success to you and to your department.

During my notice period, I will of course be pleased to provide you with any assistance you require to ensure a professional handover and to help prepare existing staff to undertake on-going projects.

Yours sincerely,

Name
Title
Department

## EXAMPLE 2 – THE EARLY LEAVER

Dear (add name of your boss),

As required by my contract of employment, I hereby give you notice of my intention to leave my position as (enter current job title).

I have decided that it is time to move on and I have accepted a position with another company. This was not an easy decision and took a lot of consideration. I am confident that my new role will help me to move towards some of the aspirations I have for my career.

I would like to start with my new employer at the earliest date and I request that you look to reduce my notice period and relieve me of my duties as soon as possible. Please be assured that I will do all I can to assist in the smooth transfer of my responsibilities before leaving.

I wish both you and (add name of present employer) every good fortune and I would like to thank you for having me as part of your team.

Yours sincerely,
XX

## EXAMPLE 3 – THE SIMPLE OPTION

Name
Address

Date

Dear (add name of your boss)

I would like to notify you that I am resigning from my position at (insert name of company) today.

I would like to thank you for my time at the firm, which I have very much enjoyed, and wish you and the company much success for the future.

Yours sincerely.

Name
Title
Department

# BODY TALK – THE UNSPOKEN LANGUAGE

*There is only this present moment. You can make a change in your life at any stage, you have to want to do it; one small step at a time.*

# BODY LANGUAGE – PART 1

........................................................

## LISTEN, WITH YOUR EYES

In 1972, Professor Albert Mehrabian published a book *Silent Messages*, in which he concluded that 93% of all communication is non-verbal. Professor Mehrabian's study showed that 55% is visual, 38% is vocal and tonal, while 7% is word only.

Once you are seated in a meeting or interview, it is time to assess where you are and observe the interviewer/s in front of you. This is where you can gauge some important telltale signs and some key indicators that may assist you through your meeting.

When reading body language you do need to allow an element of flexibility, nothing is 100%. Some people may give off a different signal, when actually they might just be cold, hot, tired or even perhaps hungry. Therefore, you need to have a certain level of judgment and make sure you do not overstep the mark in what you believe someone is or is not saying.

# MAJOR SIGNALS TO BE MINDFUL OF

## ARMS CROSSED

First and foremost, arms crossed. A number of people feel that when someone has their arms crossed, they are negative, closed off and not caring/listening. It has been highlighted that a person crossing their arms can signify them comforting themselves, similar to a hug. If someone does have their arms folded, do not take this negatively and pursue with your point regardless. Aim to highlight where you can add value to both them and the business.

## HEAD POSITION – HEAD NEUTRAL

Head position can give away a huge amount about an individual. Top poker players maintain that a head neutral position is the most optimal. It gives little indication to how your emotions are reacting to the current situation.

## THE HEAD TILT

If someone tilts their head when you are speaking it shows a level of empathy from what that person is hearing from you. Vice versa, if you use a head tilt when someone is speaking it will display the same compassionate impression.

## THE HEAD DOWN

The head down is something that you should not do. It gives a very negative, condescending and almost aggressive feeling. If you can imagine being back at school with a mean teacher looking down on you with a glaring eye, this is how you are going to be perceived. Try not to do it, unless you genuinely mean to do so.

## THE NOSE RUB

When you lie or tell mis-truths there is a chemical in your body that is released and increases the blood pressure in your nose, causing it to swell. This is according to a study conducted by scientists Dr. Alan Hirsch and Charles Wolf of The University Of Illinois. Subconsciously you want to touch, itch or rub your nose. This can be a very interesting telltale sign and one that you can hopefully learn not to do yourself.

## THE LIP AND MOUTH COVER

If you see someone cover their lips or mouth, this may mean that they are holding something back, or do not want to give something away. If you see this, you may want to dig a little deeper or try a different tack to get the person to open up. From my experience, people also hold their lips to keep themselves from interrupting when someone else is already talking.

## THE EYE RUB

If you notice a person is rubbing or closing their eyes when speaking, it is likely that they are telling you a mistruth, or they are not telling you the whole truth. With the closing and rubbing of your eyes, you are trying to keep yourself from seeing your own lies.

## THE EAR RUB

If an individual starts rubbing their ears, it can mean that they have had enough of what you are saying or at least on the topic that you are talking about. It may be that you have gone on for too long, or you are not succinct enough. Potentially they feel it is not relevant to them.

. . . . . . . . . . .

For video content on the above, please go to the
Spartan International YouTube channel:
*Body Language In Meetings – https://youtu.be/D8mN2b0pGIM

# BODY LANGUAGE – PART 2

## HOW TO IMPROVE YOUR BODY LANGUAGE IN MEETINGS

Now you are conscious of what body movements to be aware of when in front of others, here are some helpful hints and tips to improve your own body language and meeting performance.

### SIT ALL THE WAY BACK IN YOUR SEAT

As soon as you sit down, sit all the way back in your seat. This is an automatic sign of confidence and assurance. Not only will it keep your posture upright, tall and straight, it will help your vocal chords and your breathing.

### BREATHE DEEPLY AND SPEAK AS YOU EXHALE

Breathing is an extremely important part of life, let alone the interview process. Taking a deep breath can calm your nerves, settle your mind and help you focus. Additionally, when you speak on the exhale it means you have a greater length of time to speak, your sentences will not be short and your voice will be that much clearer.

## USE YOUR HANDS

If you are unsure of what to do with your hands, use them. If you talk with your hands, there is no problem in doing so. Ensure that you know where the waters and coffees are on the table, so you will not knock or spill anything. Conversely, if you do not show your hands it can often communicate a sign of dishonesty and nervousness. Aim to strike a balance.

## SHOW THE PALMS OF YOUR HANDS

Do not be afraid to use your hands whenever you are speaking. When using your hands, make sure you show your palms. Showing your palms portrays that you are ready to speak, you are open and you are honest. With the use of the palm of the hand, it can also show your energy. The energy comes from the seven chakras that run up the center of the body. It is said that the primary hand chakras are located in the center of each palm.

## DO NOT SLOUCH

It is important that you do not slouch. This is because it shows that you are bored and have no desire to be where you are. In an interview or meeting this is the last thing you want to demonstrate.

## DO NOT STARE AT THE TIME

When you keep looking at either your watch or a clock in the room, it shows that you are rude, disrespectful, impatient and can signify an ego. If you have no desire to be in that meeting, try and listen for as long as possible, try and concentrate on the other individual and do not let your eyes stray to a clock or watch.

## DO NOT MAKE EXAGGERATED GESTURES

Aim to keep your body actions within a limited range of movements. Extended or exaggerated gestures often portray that you are stretching the truth, or you are unsure of what you are saying. Try not to exaggerate a nod of your head or wild gesticulation of the hands and arms. Keep it simple, relax and speak your truth.

## WHAT TO DO WITH YOUR EYES – THE EYE ROLL

Great eye contact is a perfect combination of not avoiding eye contact and not looking too much. For the love of anything, do not roll your eyes when speaking – you know it as well as I do. When anyone sees another person roll their eyes they are automatically turned off of them.

## AVOIDING EYE CONTACT

Avoiding eye contact often signifies that you have something to hide and you are not willing to tell the truth. It can also signify a lack of confidence and insecurity. It is important that you maintain a good level of eye contact throughout any meeting or conversation. Eye contact is a good signifier of confidence in a person and in what they are saying.

## WHERE TO FOCUS

Try not to give a piercing, scowling look as it can come across as aggressive. The ideal scenario is to look somewhere around the face, ideally between the forehead and the nose. This gives the impression that you are looking directly at the person without staring too intently into their eyes.

## DO NOT CLENCH YOUR FISTS

If you have clenched fists either on the table or underneath the table, it can signify that you are not willing to listen to someone else's opinions and you will not be receptive to them. It can also come across extremely aggressively, especially if you are banging your fists on the table.

## TRY NOT TO FIDGET

Constantly playing with anything, whether it be your hair, a pen, a business card or something else shows that you are anxious or worried. Although you may not be, this is the message that you are portraying. If you are a fidgety person, put your hands together on a table or surface in front of you.

## DO NOT FORGET THE POWER OF A SMILE

Smile when appropriate; smile whenever given an opportunity to smile. Having a smile and giving a smile is one of the most positive gestures a person can receive throughout their day. You will often find that the person you have given that smile to will smile straight back at you. Try to smile, laugh and give off positive energy daily and consistently – it's a wonderful thing to be able to do.

. . . . . . . . . . .

For video content on the above, please go to the
Spartan International YouTube channel:
*Body Language Hints & Tips –
https://www.youtube.com/watch?v=rZoe9lzUX9o

# MASTERFUL GUIDANCE

*In life, things do not happen to you, they happen for you.*
*Everything happens for a reason.*

# HOW TO INCREASE YOUR VALUE AT WORK

What if the future of your job rested solely on your shoulders? To ensure your professional destiny is not dictated by anyone other than yourself, increase your value at work and take responsibility!

## KNOW WHAT IS EXPECTED OF YOU FIRST, THEN DELIVER ON WHAT IS EXPECTED

Your value is often determined by what you can deliver; these are results, in one form or another. As a matter of course, you are expected to be on time, be honest, work hard and, above all, do what your superiors ask of you in your role. Doing what is expected of you means that you are fulfilling your purpose and therefore you are valuable to the company or business. This is your very minimum level of acceptability throughout your career.

## SUPPORT YOUR BOSS

When you support your boss to achieve objectives and meet their goals and aspirations, your value as an employee will increase instantly. When you go above and beyond to assist your boss, you can expect that person to appreciate you as both a trusted employee and a friend. Those who are instrumental in attaining business objectives will be increasingly more valuable.

## BE A TEAM PLAYER

Being a team player is important in any position in any business, it is vital for the success of your company. Without active team play, you lose the ability to be pushed even further as an individual by those around you, asking you questions and helping to develop your own ideas. When you work as a team you can create something truly remarkable and powerful.

## BE MINDFUL OF OTHER PEOPLE'S EFFORTS

At times you can forget those that have helped you along the way, whether this is a teacher, former boss, colleague or friend. When you recognise the efforts of others that have benefited you in some way, small or large, you empower them and help them to develop. Not only this, they will be more likely to assist you and lend a hand in the future. Never forget the power of saying thank you and showing your appreciation.

## BE TRUTHFUL AND GIVE YOUR HONEST OPINION

Most people appreciate those who have an opinion and a view of their own. Your value will increase when you move away from being a "yes person" and give your honest and truthful opinion. Your value increases because people will automatically be able to trust you on your word. If you speak your truth, you will act on it.

## BE POSITIVE, NOT A MOANING MINNIE

In life, there is always something not to like. Something you can complain or moan about. The question is, why? No one wants to hear anyone moan about any situation, especially the pettiest little ones. It is no different within businesses. People may dislike something about a company, however, it is the way in which it is handled that is important. If you complain constantly you will reduce your value in a work place environment. Those that can remain positive and create a solution, rather than a problem, will always increase their value.

## BE WILLING TO CHANGE

Change is one of the only constants in life and in humanity. Those who are unwilling or fearful of change are likely to remain stagnant in their careers and stunt their own progression. If you can change with the times, if you can move with the evolution and revolution of industries, you will become vastly more valuable to an organisation. Always be open to change; change brought us the lightbulb, the internet and medicine. Change is good. Embrace change. Be positive for change.

## BE THE SHINING LIGHT

Be the go-to person in the company. Be the person that everyone respects and everyone wants to become. No one can quite understand how you manage to arrive before everyone, go to the gym, smash all your targets, whilst helping your teammates. Then, when the day is out, go home for dinner with your beautiful family or head out with your friends. Shine away bright star!

# CAREER CHOICES
# YOU WILL REGRET

Throughout your career you will be faced with many challenges, as well as a plethora of decisions to make. You will want to progress within your career, however, it is vital you do not fall in to some potentially detrimental pitfalls.

## PUTTING YOUR FRIENDS AND FAMILY LAST

This is something that you can struggle with, especially at the early stages of your career, and the latter as you progress. At the early stage of your career you will want to work as hard as you possibly can and climb the corporate ladder as quickly as you can, whilst trying to impress everyone you can. As you go through the latter end of your career and you come to a management position, time becomes more and more elusive and harder to manage. That said, it is imperative to keep your friends and family close. These are the people that will always support you through everything in life, regardless of your job and anything that happens in it. Never forget that without these individuals, life becomes fairly meaningless. Without friends and family to support you, to talk to you, to discuss or even enjoy the successes that you are having, what is the point? Make sure you do not leave yourself empty and lonely. Pay respect to those around you.

## SETTLING FOR LESS

Settling in the job you are in, the money you are receiving, the company you are working for. There are so many versions of settling, it is important to always believe in yourself. Your self-belief means that you do not have to settle, it means that you can achieve and your intuition will guide you to exactly where you need to be. You are often given what you need rather than what you want, however, to settle is something you should never do in your life or career.

## MAKING DECISIONS PURELY BASED ON MONEY

There is no question about the fact that you need to live, you need to earn and you need to pay your bills. There is always stress, there is always dis-ease. You will always get through it as long as you work hard and smart.

When making career decisions purely based on money, you could be enticed to move at any point for a higher financial package – no one could blame you. When you make decisions based on money, you take out the softer factors; the factors that could potentially be more important to you and for you. For example: the culture of the company, where the role is based, will you be working long hours, will you be able to see your family, is it a position that motivates you? There are a vast number of reasons not to base your career decisions on money – LOOK AT THE BIGGER PICTURE! Assess how the move will impact you and your loved ones. What fulfils you internally will mean so much more to you as you progress through life.

## NOT FOCUSING ON YOUR PASSION

Those that focus on their passion are more likely to be successful and contented in their careers. When you find your passion, you deliver at a higher and more energetic level. Having passion in your career completely merges your job into your life, becoming one unified entity. It becomes something you love and look forward to every single day. Your passion combines your life into one. You become the person you have desired to be.

## THINKING ONLY OF YOURSELF

It is clear that you are going to look after yourself in your career; if you do not, who will? It can be difficult for anyone to look outside of themselves within their job. When doing so, it is important to look at the greater good. If you are in a team and you can help that team advance, it is worthwhile looking at the whole rather than at the sum of its parts. You might find that looking out for others or seeing other people's perspectives can be alien to you. When you are part of a team, that is when you can be even better than yourself. Being a part of something far greater, something far more magical.

**To know and to understand your true desires will ensure that these regrets will not happen to you.**

. . . . . . . . . . .

For video content on the above, please go to the
Spartan International YouTube channel:
*Career Choices You Will Regret – https://youtu.be/hBlkOLFAy2A

# HABITS TO BE HIGHLY SUCCESSFUL

..............................................................

Throughout your career, you can often look at successful people and wonder how they achieve such success and where they get their mentality from. Here are some of the most vital habits to follow in order to start achieving success.

## FOCUS ON WHAT YOU CAN CONTROL, NOT WHAT YOU CANNOT

You may have heard the saying, "do not worry about what you cannot control". This is exactly what successful people do, they focus on what is in their world and what they can actually do something about.

## LEARN FROM YOUR MISTAKES

Do not make one mistake and continuously make the same mistake over and over again. Successful people listen, learn, progress and move on.

## TAKE RESPONSIBILITY

Successful people take responsibility for everything in their lives. They do not evade blame or pass responsibility. They accept every opportunity, every challenge, every mistake and own it. This is something that fully self-confident people do, if you do not act in this manner you will always avoid taking responsibility.

## MAKE PEACE WITH YOUR PAST

There is no question you will go through ups and downs in your life, sometimes difficult and sometimes damaging. However, successful people will look at their past, look at the experiences they have had and take the positives from them. Not only that, they are willing to take it one step further forward and make it their own. They completely take command of what happened. They accept it, learn from the experience and then use those lessons to better themselves and to guide others.

## SET ASIDE TIME TO BE ALONE

Successful people always set aside time to be alone. This is often to be alone with their thoughts, to think through the day, plan for the future and to meditate. Spending time meditating will calm your thoughts and assists you to be centred. Taking time for yourself is also a signal of high emotional intelligence (EQ).

## ALWAYS TAKE CALCULATED RISKS

Successful people always take calculated risks. Stepping outside your comfort zone and seeking opportunities are absolutely imperative for success. Taking a calculated risk is far more advisable than putting it all on black or red at a roulette table in a casino, and hoping it comes up.

## DEFINE SUCCESS YOUR OWN WAY

Successful people always define success in their own way and will focus on what they want to achieve. This means that they do not let other people's success and achievements diminish their own. This usually comes from a higher place and a willingness to do more for the world than for themselves. This is true success and achievement, your achievement.

## BE BOTH POSITIVE AND REALISTIC

If you view every day and opportunity with a positive outlook, you are likely to see an outlook that is going to benefit yourself, your business and those around you. It is important you take a realistic approach in everything you do in life. Do not live with your head in the clouds.

## STAY TRUE TO YOUR CORE VALUES

Core values are what you live by, what you believe in and the ethical lines you will not cross. This is so that you are not influenced by those around you, the world at large and by any negativity that comes your way. It is staying true to who you are, no matter whether it is popular opinion or not. It is who you are to your core.

## SIX WORDS THAT LEAD TO SUCCESS

If you *WORK HARD*, with *LOGIC, PROCESS, CONTINUITY* and *CONSISTENCY*, you will be successful, in anything.

. . . . . . . . . . .

For video content on the above, please go to the
Spartan International YouTube channel:
*Habits of Highly Successful People –
https://www.youtube.com/watch?v=CzrsNdeg80c

# HOW TO BE AN UNFORGETTABLE LEADER

.........................................................

Throughout history there have been some particularly influential leaders. These have come in the shape of Sir Winston Churchill, Abraham Lincoln, Napoleon Bonaparte and many more. Shape yourself to be the best leader you can possibly become.

## PROTECT YOUR TEAM

Guide those around you and take responsibility for them. Bosses that run away from the responsibility of leading a team often find themselves in difficulty later down the road. Not only that, the loyalty of their team is likely to diminish over time. Your position is to protect them: protect your team. Guide them and empower them. By doing this you are helping to establish loyalty and a team that is sustainable and committed for the long haul.

## LEAD BY PERMISSION, NOT BY FORCE OR AUTHORITY

Rather than dictating to your team and to those around you, lead by guidance and lead by questioning. If you have a new idea that you want to pursue, discuss this with the team and assess what the response is. When doing so, it is recommended not to give them your answer before you have asked their opinion. In doing this you completely negate the exercise and tell them exactly what you want to hear. It is likely that you will then hear the same response in different variations. If you lead by permission, you are always going to follow the greater good of your team and have a collaborative approach. Empower your team!

## BELIEVE IN THE IMPOSSIBLE

Great bosses tend to believe in the unbelievable, unachievable and unimaginable. Believing in the achievable is believing in what you can see, use and follow. Believing in the impossible is believing in breaking new ground and walking the path less travelled. They utilise all that is available and at their disposal. There are no limits, only those that you impose on yourself.

## BELIEVE IN THE GREATER GOOD

If you take the likes of Steve Jobs or Elon Musk, these individuals have looked at the greater good for all of us, as well as how to advance technology, progress the world and give us a more sustainable future. The greater good is you giving back to the rest of mankind and progressing the human race in your own unique way. Of course, there is no one specific way to do this. Be creative, be free and break barriers.

## LOOK AT OPPORTUNITIES WITHIN INSTABILITY

In this world of constant change, many are panicked, scared and worried about themselves. Great leaders will look at this time as a great opportunity to progress. When there is sizable change in an industry, there are always a vast array of opportunities that surface. This is where an unforgettable boss will undoubtedly strive, stand out and show their key attributes. With their passion, determination and purpose they will get their team and all those around them marching to the beat of their drum. This is an impressive skill, one that is immeasurably important. This only comes with dedication, passion, understanding and experience.

## WEAR YOUR HEART ON YOUR SLEEVE

No one expects to see their boss crying at their desk or weeping through the office. This is about empathy, understanding and a willingness to listen to your team and those around you. Whilst it is inappropriate for physical contact in the work place, find a way to put a non-physical arm around the shoulder of anyone that needs it; give some hints, tips and guidance that will help to get them through tough moments.

## TWO WORDS – THANK AND YOU

These two words seem extremely simple to say – although it is not as easy as you would think. How many times have you gone to a superior after doing the work they have asked you to do and they have not even bothered to say thank you? A simple thank you is all it takes for you to empower your team. Saying thank you is very easy to do and is something you may often forget – you must not. An individual is likely to feel happier and more respected if after they have finished a piece of work for you, you simply say, "Thank you, I appreciate your effort."

# LEGENDARY QUOTES

In your career it is likely that you will look for guidance from those who have been in your position beforehand, or that can offer some specific words of wisdom to assist you on your journey. Highlighted below are some truly memorable and inspiring quotes for you to utilise when you need a boost throughout your career. (All quotes are available from multiple sources, including YouTube and the internet).

### MICHAEL JORDAN
### LEGENDARY BASKETBALL PLAYER

Basketball legend Michael Jordan said, **"Earn your leadership every single day."** As a championship basketball player, it is easy to understand why he thinks this way. No one should be given leadership, it is something that is earned. The way in which you earn it is leading by example, listening to others, helping others and by elevating and empowering others.

### STEVE JOBS
### LEGENDARY TECHNOLOGY PIONEER

Steve Jobs said, **"My job is not to be easy on people. My job is to take these great people we have and to push them and make them even better."** Using a sports analogy, I believe that many professional sports coaches do this. Daily, weekly, monthly and yearly they get the extra 1-2% out of people, this is by psychologically or physically improving an individual. Steve Jobs was no different, he wanted that from his team, from his company and has left a phenomenal legacy.

## HENRY FORD
### LEGENDARY AUTOMOTIVE PIONEER

One of my favourite quotes comes from Henry Ford. Mr Ford said, **"You do not have to hold a position in order to be a leader."** This is a quote I love. I believe in many respects, some of us are born leaders and some of us develop to be leaders. Whether you hold a position of leadership or not, you can still lead by example; you can still be a shining light and let others follow your lead. Always do the right thing, always follow your passion and follow your intuition.

## VINCE LOMBARDI
### LEGENDARY AMERICAN FOOTBALL COACH

This is a fantastic American football coach who is one of the most decorated of all time, Vince Lombardi, who said, **"Leaders are not born, they are made."** They are made like anything else, through sheer hard work. Whether it is Alex Ferguson, Vince Lombardi, Pep Guardiola or Bill Belichick, you know the mentality that these men have; you can tell that they get the very last ounce out of everyone they work with. They expect the best from themselves and everyone around them.

## MR J.P. MORGAN
### LEGENDARY BANKING PIONEER

Mr. J.P. Morgan said, **"A man always has two reasons for doing anything: a good reason and the real reason."** It is understanding what Mr Morgan is saying that will help us elevate ourselves. There are usually two reasons for what you do in life, one is invariably for ourselves and those around us. The other... for the greater good of humanity. As you are motivated to perform positive deeds for the greater good, it will come back to you in your life, in one form or another. So maybe there are two reasons for your motivations, consciously or subconsciously.

## SIR RICHARD BRANSON
### LEGENDARY SERIAL ENTREPRENEUR

Sir Richard Branson is famous for his eccentric ways, his fantastic leadership skills and being slightly quirky, if not completely off the wall. This is a great quote from Sir Richard, **"Screw it, let's do it."** I love this quote because it highlights the fact that you should give it a go, whatever it is. If it does not work, you can stop it, start again, or in the worst case – scrap it. At the very least, give it a try before giving up!

. . . . . . . . . . .

For video content on the above, please go to the
Spartan International YouTube channel:
*Leadership Quotes – https://youtu.be/UblY_cjwO5c

# INSPIRING QUOTES

Sometimes we all need an occasional pick me up or pep talk. The following quotes will have you running around your office and beating your chest in no time. Suit up and strap on! (All quotes are available from multiple sources, including YouTube and the internet).

▶ *"You can't connect the dots looking forward; you can only connect them looking backwards. So you have to trust that the dots will somehow connect in your future. You have to trust in something: your gut, destiny, life, karma, whatever. Because believing that the dots will connect down the road will give you the confidence to follow your heart even when it leads you off the well worn path; and that will make all the difference."* — **Steve Jobs**

▶ *"Human happiness and human satisfaction must ultimately come from within oneself."* — **Dalai Lama**

▶ *"Remember to look up at the stars and not down at your feet. Try to make sense of what you see and wonder about what makes the universe exist. Be curious. And however difficult life may seem, there is always something you can do and succeed at. It matters that you don't just give up."* — **Stephen Hawking**

▶ *"When I was five years old, my mother always told me that happiness was the key to life. When I went to school, they asked me what I wanted to be when I grew up. I wrote down 'happy'. They told me I didn't understand the assignment, and I told them they didn't understand life."* — **John Lennon**

▶ *"If you can't fly, run. If you can't run, walk. If you can't walk, crawl. No matter what, keep moving."* — **Martin Luther King, Jr.**

▶ *"We are going to relentlessly chase perfection, knowing full well we will not catch it, because nothing is perfect. But we are going to relentlessly chase it, because in the process we will catch excellence."* – **Vince Lombardi**

▶ *"It takes 20 years to build a reputation and five minutes to ruin it. If you think about that, you'll do things differently"* – **Warren Buffett**

▶ *"Build your own dreams, or someone else will hire you to build theirs."* — **Farrah Gray**

▶ *"Nothing is impossible, the word itself says 'I'm possible'!"* — **Audrey Hepburn**

▶ *"I never lose. I either win or I learn."* – **Nelson Mandela**

▶ *"Being entirely honest with oneself is a good exercise"* – **Sigmund Freud**

▶ *"If you look at what you have in life, you'll always have more. If you look at what you don't have in life, you'll* never have enough." — **Oprah Winfrey**

▶ "Strive not to be a success, but rather to be of value."
— **Albert Einstein**

▶ "Don't judge each day by the harvest you reap but by
the seeds that you plant." — **Robert Louis Stevenson**

▶ "If you hear a voice within you say 'you cannot paint',
then by all means paint and that voice will be silenced."
— **Vincent Van Gogh**

▶ "Whatever the mind of man can conceive and believe,
it can achieve." — **Napoleon Hill**

▶ "It is during our darkest moments that we must focus
to see the light." — **Aristotle Onassis**

▶ "What's money? A man is a success if he gets up in
the morning and goes to bed at night and in between
does what he wants to do." — **Bob Dylan**

▶ "I am not a product of my circumstances. I am a
product of my decisions." — **Stephen Covey**

▶ "How wonderful it is that nobody need wait a single
moment before starting to improve the world." — **Anne
Frank**

▶ "Certain things catch your eye, but pursue only those
that capture the heart." — **Ancient Indian Proverb**

▶ "What we achieve inwardly will change outer reality."
— **Plutarch**

▶ *"Death is stripping away of all that is not you. The secret of life is to 'die before you die' – and find that there is no death." –* **Eckhart Tolle**

▶ *"The whole secret of a successful life is to find out what is one's destiny to do, and then do it" –* **Henry Ford**

## THE PERSONAL TOUCH – A FEW FROM ME

▶ *Love like you mean it, laugh like you mean it and work like you mean it. Do not live an average life, living like a zombie, not actually living. Do what you want to be doing, what your heart and soul truly desires.*

▶ *Every experience in life is either a chance to progress and learn, or to repeat past lessons missed. The more you experience and learn, the more you can assist and guide others. We are all one people.*

▶ *What you want in life is not often what you need. Life often grants you with your needs and does not care for what you believe you do not have.*

▶ *Live your life. Do not live your life through others. Do you, there is only one of you. You are an original, do not be a fake!*

▶ *Be careful what you say to someone today because you may not have tomorrow to take it back.*

▶ *You only live once – wrong! You live every day and die once. Do not waste today.*

# A BETTER YOU

*Find your passion.*
*Find your focus.*
*Free yourself, and have fun whilst doing it.*

# HOW TO BE A MORE POSITIVE PERSON

In life, you will always have ups and downs, however, in a study by Shawn Achor (a Harvard researcher), it has been found that having a positive mentality can increase sales by a colossal 37%, your productivity by an outstanding 31% and increased accuracy on tasks by 19%! That alone is enough to start thinking positively.

## BE THE MASTER OF YOUR KINGDOM

You and you alone are the master of your destiny and life. Whilst you will always have people of influence (parents, bosses, friends etc.) giving their guidance, it is important to listen to yourself and your intuition. You are the only person who really knows you and understands you.

## THERE ARE NO PROBLEMS, ONLY SOLUTIONS

You will face situations and challenges every single day of your life, especially in the working world. It is key to change your inner narrative and look at every situation with a positive outlook. Only focus on the solutions, not the problems.

## LIVE A HEALTHY LIFESTYLE

Eat well, sleep between six to eight hours a night, drink at least a litre and a half of water daily, get some exercise every day (even a brisk 10-15 minute walk), listen to music and take time to either meditate or be alone and reflect on yourself. Give yourself time to breathe, mentally and physically.

## ALWAYS BE PRESENT

When speaking with anyone, either on the phone, in person or via video conference, always be present. Do not be distracted by the sights and sounds around you. Do not get distracted by mobile devices beeping and buzzing. Focus on the person you are speaking with and listen to their every word. They will remember you fondly and will always be open to further conversations.

## SAY WHAT YOU MEAN AND
## MEAN WHAT YOU SAY

To live a truly happy life you must think, speak and act in unison. When you pretend or act in a way to please others, you are denying your true self and therefore living a lie. In life, and in work, it is alright to say "no", or "not at the moment". It is when you say "yes" and mean "no" there becomes an internal conflict. Be true to yourself, say what you mean and mean what you say.

## THERE IS NO COMPARISON

In a world that is heavily laden with social media, pretty people and everyone seemingly a billionaire, it is truly important not to fall into the trap of comparing yourself or your life with others. Being happy with who you truly are means that you will never have to look outside of yourself for a contented life. You do not need other people's acceptance and approval for you to be important and unique. You are always that.

## SAY IT TO THEIR FACE, NOT THEIR BACK

Should a situation arise whereby you need to confront someone for one reason or another, do not spend your time bad-mouthing or back-stabbing that individual first. Be brave, non-confrontational and aim to work out a way forward for you both to assist each other. If that does not work, aim to make clear guidelines you can both mutually agree on and stick to.

## ALWAYS LOOK AT OTHER PEOPLE'S PERSPECTIVES

Being able to look at someone else's point of view will immediately assist you in everyday life. Understanding what someone else's motivations are can be the key to a successful and mutually agreeable negotiation.

## YOU EITHER WIN OR YOU LEARN

Taking risks both personally and professionally does not come naturally to everyone. We all want to know if we will succeed before trying. Whatever you do, you will either win or you will learn. You will never lose!

## WAIT YOUR TURN AND LISTEN INTENTLY

Being able to listen to someone, internalise what they are saying, whilst keeping quiet without letting your thoughts come out... is not as easy as it sounds. Listening helps you absorb the wisdom and experience of others. When you are able to understand what someone is saying, you can show an understanding and empathy towards them. They will automatically warm to you.

## ALWAYS LOOK AT THE BIGGER PICTURE

Looking at the bigger picture can help in many ways. In a negotiation it can always assist in maintaining future positive relationships. It has no boundaries and you are free to create and explore all avenues of your mind. The best minds in humanity always thought BIG. Shoot for the stars and you may land on the moon!

## APPRECIATE WHAT YOU HAVE

Being able to appreciate what you have in life is one of the most important and self-fulfilling acts anyone can achieve. Being able to appreciate the absolute simplicity of life is the very essence of our existence. Breathe deeply, think clearly and enjoy the present moment, for it is the only one that exists.

# IMPROVE YOUR CORE ENERGY

......................................................

Having a solid core energy base is vitally important to your wellbeing and focus at all times. If you do not look after and feed your core, you are likely to perform at a suboptimum level. Give yourself the best chance of success, look after yourself and your wellbeing.

## GET A GOOD NIGHT'S SLEEP

First and foremost, and one of the most obvious points for core energy, is a great night's sleep. Having between six and eight hours will leave you completely rested and ready for a new day. That being said, having a disturbed six to eight hours is not the same thing and therefore you must look for a complete, undisturbed and rested night's sleep. If you start to go to bed earlier and wake up earlier, you will feel fresher, brighter and more alive. You will certainly have that extra 1-2% of energy.

## EXERCISE DAILY

Another immediate highlight for core energy is exercise. Exercising daily is absolutely imperative and will help you get a great start to the day. Exercising in the morning will help increase adrenalin, which will also help with stamina for the rest of the day.

## REDUCE YOUR MATERIALISTIC LIFESTYLE

Being constantly surrounded by material objects can be overbearing and suffocating. If you can live your life with only what you need, rather than what you want, you will be internally more positive, more contented and with a far clearer headspace. Thus, improving your core energy.

## DRESS TO IMPRESS

You know that dressing to impress makes you feel more confident. When you wear your best suit, shirt, dress or skirt, you will always give that extra 1-2%. It is in how you feel. This genuinely comes with confidence. If you look good, you feel good. Additionally, other people will notice this as well and will send you positive energy in response.

## SURROUND YOURSELF WITH LIKE-MINDED PEOPLE

Surrounding yourself with people that are positive and like-minded is key for a calm and contented lifestyle. Clearing away people that have a negative impact on your life is very important, although it can sometimes be extremely difficult to do. It must be done. If you surround yourself with positive people you will start to feel that positivity back. If you do surround yourself with negative energy you are likely to make your core energy lower rather than higher.

## FOCUS ON YOUR GOALS

Focus on your goals so much so that you write them down on a daily basis and recite them both in the morning and in the evening. If you recite these every morning you will start the new day fresh, bright and ready to go. By reciting these every evening you will clarify your thoughts and focus on what is important and carry that message forward to the new day coming.

. . . . . . . . . . .

For video content on the above, please go to the
Spartan International YouTube channel:
*Core Energy – How to Improve – https://youtu.be/aXdzFRkJw1k

# MEDITATION AND DEEP BREATHING

Meditation seems to be everywhere around us at present. From Buddhist monks to the most well-known and revered CEOs, celebrities and sportspeople on the planet. A vast number of people feel the benefits and personal development from meditation.

## BENEFITS OF MEDITATION AND DEEP BREATHING

### FEEL AGELESS AND MORE BEAUTIFUL

Breathing deeply slows the aging process by increasing secretion of anti-aging hormones! By reducing stress, it improves your mood, elevating the levels of serotonin and endorphins.

### FREE YOURSELF FROM PAIN

When you deep breathe through meditation, the body releases endorphins, which are the feel good hormones and a natural painkiller created by the body itself. It has also been said that deep breathing reduces inflammation in the body, this is due to the reduction of acid in your body from the decrease of stress in your life through your meditations.

## FEEL ALIVE

When meditating on a regular basis, your blood flow will increase, which means that you are getting more oxygen into your bloodstream. The result of this additional oxygen is increased energy levels.

## TAKE A MOMENT TO RELAX

Meditation is one of the most peaceful, relaxing and magical exercises anyone can achieve. With practice and patience, meditation can reset your mind, whilst experiencing peace, calm and serenity all at once. German psychiatrist, Johannes Heinrich Schultz, developed a deep breathing method of relaxation that is still one of the best-known Western relaxation techniques today – Autogenic Training. To enjoy a complete moment of calm...is to enjoy a moment of bliss.

## IMPROVE YOUR FOCUS

There have been a number of studies undertaken globally, whereby the results all show that with regular deep breathing your focus, attention and psychomotor functions all improve. When you meditate you stimulate the pre-frontal cortex, this is the part of the brain responsible for concentration and problem solving.

## CONTROL YOUR EMOTIONS

If you are ever overcome by emotion, being able to have control over your breathing will enable you to take steady, calm, deep breaths, bringing you back in control of yourself positively. With regular practice you can take control of your emotions at will.

## EXPAND YOUR MEMORY

It has been found that with regular deep breathing, using a technique called "deep alternate-nostril breathing", your memory recall can increase significantly.

## CALM YOUR NERVES AND EASE WORRIES

Deep breathing or meditation exercises reduce stress and anxiety. Whether this is done regularly, or at the time you need it most; being able to take five to seven clear, slow, long, deep breaths will calm your nerves and give you a moment of clarity.

## START ON THE PATH TO ENLIGHTENMENT

Meditation can take many different forms, from simple deep breathing to the Buddhist monks seeking enlightenment. Mediation is found in many, if not all, religions, in one form or another. These can include the reciting of prayers or repetition of mantras daily. The goal is to achieve an altered state of consciousness with the intention of connecting with a higher deity.

The more time you can find to meditate the more aware you will become of what your wants and needs truly are; what lies beneath, the true version of yourself. Regular meditation gives rise to clarity about what is important in life and a sense of confidence to make choices that ignite your passions and dissolve distractions. Suddenly a new world is opened to you, and it is completely different. Life takes on greater meaning and you feel a deeper sense of purpose and contentment.

# DEEP BREATHING AND MEDITATION EXERCISES

· · · · · · · · · · · · · · · · · · · · · · · · · · · · · · · · · · · · · · · · · · · · ·

Using my personal experiences, I have outlined a step-by-step guide to a simple deep breathing exercise and a more detailed meditation. This is a simple guide to get you started. Enjoy your moment and look forward to the peace, calm and serenity of meditation.

## DEEP BREATHING EXERCISE

### A SIMPLE HOW-TO DEEP BREATHING GUIDE

▶ *Either lying down, sitting or standing*

▶ *You can choose to open or close your eyes*

▶ *With your mouth closed*

▶ *Take a slow, steady inwards breath through your nose*

▶ *Allow your diaphragm and ribcage to expand as your lungs fill with air*

▶ *Once your lungs are fully expanded, hold for three to five seconds*

▶ *Exhale slowly through your mouth until you have no air left in your lungs*

▶ *Stop, and start again*

▶ *Continue this for five to ten minutes, or as long as you feel you need*

▶ *Build up your time slowly and enjoy this moment!*

## MEDITATION EXERCISE

### A HOW-TO MEDITATION GUIDE

▶ *Set some specific time aside to meditate, time just for you. Allow yourself a set amount of time (ten to thirty minutes to begin with).*

▶ *If you can set a fixed time daily, or a weekly schedule, this will help keep the time available for you and will encourage you to look forward to this moment*

▶ *Before you begin, make sure you are comfortable*

▶ *Wear comfortable clothing, nothing that will annoy, impede or irritate you. I would also suggest taking off rings, watches and bracelets as these can impede your clarity and can cause distraction*

▶ *It is a good idea to have some water nearby for before and after your meditation*

▶ Some people enjoy meditation music, if you do, now is the time to put this on (make sure it does not have adverts, especially when streaming online)

▶ It is possible to meditate in both low and natural light. Find what you feel most comfortable and relaxed with

▶ Find a comfortable place to sit that is warm and where you will not be distracted. Feeling totally at ease and relaxed

▶ Relax your body before you begin and let everything hang loose

▶ Close your eyes and be aware of the space around you

▶ Take a moment to notice the sounds, temperature, feeling of the room and how you feel

▶ Clear your mind and set your intention for the meditation. Do you want to de-stress? Find an answer to a question? Take time for yourself?

▶ Say it three times in your mind

▶ When you are ready to begin, take a long, deep breath through your nose. All the while keeping your mouth closed

▶ Allow your diaphragm and ribcage to expand as your lungs fill with air

▶ *Once your lungs are fully expanded, hold for three to five seconds*

▶ *Exhale slowly through your mouth until you have no air left in your lungs*

▶ *Stop, and start again*

▶ *Do not worry about whether you are doing it "the right way", look forward to this moment and focus solely on your breathing*

▶ *As you continue you will start to feel more relaxed*

▶ *On your fourth or fifth breath, imagine that you have a beautiful, warm, beaming ray of light above your head (it can help to imagine bright sunlight)*

▶ *When you take in a breath from now on, see and feel that beautiful, warm, golden ray of light being breathed in to your body. All the way from your head, right the way down to your toes and through to the ground (imagine being bathed internally in beautiful sunlight)*

▶ *Take some time to enjoy this moment and feeling. Continue with your breathing as you relax more and more*

▶ *As you immerse yourself in the meditation, you may feel as if your mind has separated from your physical body. In this moment, you are able to assess your inner being. Realise that all is calm in this moment*

▶ *At this time, you can send messages of positivity, health and success to yourself from an altered, higher state*

▶ *Imagine yourself in your future vision. Imagine yourself fully healthy, being promoted or having a family. Whatever you decide to choose at this time*

▶ *Enjoy being in this moment, this is your time*

▶ *As you continue your breathing, be aware of your surroundings, of how you feel*

▶ *When you feel that you are ready to end your meditation, start taking normal breaths*

▶ *Start to bring your conscious back to the room or space you are sitting in*

▶ *Wiggle your fingers and toes to help bring yourself back to the room*

▶ *When you feel alert and ready, open your eyes. Give yourself some time to adjust to the light*

▶ *Take a drink of water to replenish yourself (staying hydrated is very important after a meditation)*

▶ *As soon as you have finished, stand up and move on with the day ahead, with great positivity.*

# THE FINAL WORD

*You are the director of your life.*
*Live in the present moment.*
*Find your passion and take action today.*

# THE FINALE

Looking around there seems only confusion and madness.
Here's to your career, may it bring only gladness.

Do not look to the dark, but instead to light.
Never give up the hardest of fights.

Life is a journey for one and for all,
how you live it can make you stand tall.

Do not follow the crowd, instead, follow your feet.
Live your life to the sounds of your own heartbeat.

Your career can be tough, painful in places.
We accept what's been before us,
as this was God's graces.

On to the next, full of hope and belief.
Ahead full of promise and nothing but peace.

With family and team right by our side,
we promise to stand strong and never to hide.

With love and support giving strength to believe,
we know what must be done to follow our dreams.

We devote our lives to the ones we love,
with guidance and strength from the powers above.

To those that have wronged, it is never too late,
to put others first and save your own fate.

Be no preacher, no Merlin, or no magician – we are one
people, on our own solitary mission.

To one and to all, and to all a great career.
Go to the future with positivity, and with no fear.

Good luck in everything you do.
Be the best version of yourself.

Be positive every day.

**Be a Survivor!**

# VIDEO GUIDANCE –
# VIA YOUTUBE

..............................................................

All of these videos are online now! Click or use the links below for the Spartan International YouTube channel, as well as all the videos that relate to the chapters in this guide – plus a couple of special editions.

### Spartan International YouTube Channel:
https://www.youtube.com/channel/
UCXUsivOw74UZpsN9Oclhy3w

Introduction:
https://youtu.be/6NC4dvVuSMo

*Simple Steps to Formatting Your CV
https://youtu.be/UiDU62ua-64

*Why Your CV Is Not Getting You The Job You Want
https://youtu.be/EGnfBkdX_oM

*Handshakes And What They Mean
https://youtu.be/xSnsWtSPmTg

*How to Survive The Interview Process
https://youtu.be/4jPrlo6xE-E

*Interview Questions And What They Mean
https://youtu.be/oOlyW48i9aY

*Phone Interviews
https://youtu.be/S5Xztu07ERE

*Body Language In Meetings
https://youtu.be/D8mN2b0pGIM

*Habits of Highly Successful People
https://www.youtube.com/watch?v=CzrsNdeg80c

*Career Choices You Will Regret
https://youtu.be/hBlk0LFAy2A

*Leadership Quotes
https://youtu.be/UblY_cjwO5c

*Core Energy — How to Improve —
https://youtu.be/aXdzFRkJw1k

*Get Out in The Open
https://youtu.be/fee587Wc1lE

# CONTACT US

Should you wish to know more about our services, whether this is Life and Career Coaching or Global Executive Search, contact us at:

Spartan International Executive Search

survivorstoday@spartan-exec.com
www.spartan-int.com

+44 203 372 5070 – London
+1 646 688 2393 – New York


## FOLLOW US:

Linkedin: Spartan International Executive Search

Twitter: @SpartanInt

YouTube: Spartan International Executive Search

# BIBLIOGRAPHY

Brain Twisting Questions, all available for reference on the internet: Brainscape, Brainly, Quizlet, iBankingFAQ and more, *Page 38*

Mind Bending Questions, all available for reference on the internet: Brainscape, Brainly, Quizlet, iBankingFAQ and more, *Pages 40-43*

Professor Albert Mehrabian — *Silent Messages,* 1972, *page 71*

Scientists Dr Alan Hirsch and Charles Wolf of The University Of Illinois, Study on Bill Clinton, *page 73*

Harvard researcher Shawn Achor — *The Happiness Advantage*, 2010, *page 107*

Psychiatrist Johannes Heinrich Schult — Hypnose-Technik, 1965, *page 116*

*Personal Quotes, all are available for reference from multiple sources, including YouTube & the internet:*

Michael Jordan, *page 98*
*As quoted in the Motivational, Inspirational and Success Quotes — To Get Motivated Every Day (2013) by Luna Belle*

Steve Jobs, *page 98 & 101*
*Stanford University. "Text of Steve Jobs' Commencement Address (2005)." Stanford News, 12 June 2017*

*Interview with Fortune Senior Editor Betsy Morris in February 2008 in Kona, Hawaii*

Henry Ford, *page 99 & 104*
*As quoted in Leading So People Will Follow by Erika Andersen (2012)*

*Henry Ford (1922). "Ford Ideals: Being a Selection from "Mr. Ford's Page" in The Dearborn Independent"*

Vince Lombardi, *page 99 & 102*
*As quoted in The Executioner: Implementing Intangible, Elusive Success Principals (2014) by Artie McFerrin*

*First team meeting as Packers coach (1959), reported in Chuck Carlson, Game of My Life: 25 Stories of Packers Football (2004), p. 149; Richard Scott, Jay Barker, Legends of Alabama Football (2004), p. 78.*

Mr J.P. Morgan, *page 100*
*In 1930 the memoir "Roosevelt: The Story of a Friendship" by Owen Wister was published*

Sir Richard Branson, *page 100*
*As quoted in Screw It, Let's Do It: Lessons In Life (2011) by Sir Richard Branson*

Stephen Hawking, *page 101*
*As quoted in Brief Answers to the Big Questions: The Final Book from Stephen Hawking (2018) by Stephen Hawking*

Dalai Lama, *page 101*
*The Path to Tranquillity: Daily Wisdom (1998) edited by Renuka Singh*

John Lennon, *page 102*
*As quoted in Simple Suggestions to Nourish the Mind, Body, and Spirit (2016)*

Martin Luther King, *page XIII & 102*
*"Keep Moving from this Mountain" – Founders Day Address at the Sisters Chapel, Spelman College (11 April 1960)*

Farrah Gray, *page 102*
*As quoted in Golden Words: 365 Quotations – A good Thought for a day by Anand Singh Mehra*

Audrey Hepburn, *page 102*
*Audrey Hepburn: How to Be Lovely: The Audrey Hepburn Way of Life (Hardcover); 2004 Edition*

Sigmund Freud, *page 102*
*Letter to Wilhelm Fliess (15 October 1897), as quoted in Origins of Psychoanalysis*

Warren Buffett, *page 102*
*Interview in Forbes magazine (1 November 1974)*

Nelson Mandela, *page 102*
*As quoted in Lawyering from the Inside Out: Learning Professional Development Through Mindfulness and Emotional Intelligence (2018) by Nathalie Martin*

Oprah Winfrey, *page 102/3*
*As quoted in The Pie Life: A Guilt-Free Recipe For Success and Satisfaction (2016) by Samantha Ettus*

Albert Einstein, *page 103*
*As quoted in The Quotable Einstein (1996) by Albert Einstein: Edited by Alice Calaprice*

Robert Louis Stevenson, *page 103*
*As quoted in Imperfect Spirituality: Extraordinary Enlightenment for Ordinary People (2012) by Polly Campbell*

Vincent Van Gogh, *page 103*
*As quoted in The Path to Tranquility: Daily Wisdom (1998) edited by Renuka Singh*

Napoleon Hill, *page 103*
*As quoted in Self-Motivation Through Risk Taking!: Are You Leading Or Do You Wither with Problems? (2005) by M. Nadarajan Munisamy*

Aristotle Onassis, *page 103*
*As quoted by $500,000* Worth of Inspiring Quotations for Our Times (2011) by Web Augustine*

Bob Dylan, *page 103*
*As quoted in Work Smarts: What CEOs Say You Need To Know To Get Ahead (2013) by B. Liu*

Stephen Covey, *page 103*
*As quoted in The Ultimate Book of Powerful Quotations: 510 Quotes About Wisdom, Love and Success by Robin Sacredfire*

Anne Frank, *page 103*
*As quoted in Tales from The Secret Annex (1949) revised (2003) by Anne Frank*

Ancient Indian Proverb, *page 103*
*Conversations with My Soul: Stories and reflections on life, death, and love after loss by Ellen P. Fitzkee*

Plutarch, *page 103*
*As quoted in Organisational Behaviour (2013) by Afsaneah Nahavandi, Robert B. Deanhardt, Janet V. Denhardt and Maria P. Aristigueta*

Eckhart Tolle, *page 104*
*As quoted in The Power of Now: A Guide to Spiritual Enlightenment (2004) by Eckhart Tolle*

# THE DISCLAIMER

........................................................

This book is presented solely for educational, motivational and entertainment purposes. The author and publisher are not offering it as legal, psychological, or other professional services advice. While best efforts have been used in preparing this book, the author and publisher make no representations or warranties of any kind and assume no liabilities of any kind with respect to the accuracy or completeness of the contents and specifically disclaim any implied warranties of merchantability or fitness of use for a particular purpose. Neither the publisher nor the author shall be liable for any physical, psychological, emotional, financial, or commercial damages, including, but not limited to, special, incidental, consequential or other damages or responsible to any person or entity with respect to any loss or incidental or consequential damages caused, or alleged to have been caused, directly or indirectly, by the information or programs contained herein. No warranty may be created or extended by sales representatives or written sales materials. Every company is different and the advice and strategies contained herein may not be suitable for your situation. You should seek the services of a competent professional before beginning any improvement program. Our views and rights are the same: you are responsible for your own choices, actions and results.

YOUR CAREER. YOUR LIFE. YOUR DECISION.

# NOTES

# NOTES

# NOTES

# NOTES